Irreverent Persia

IRANIAN STUDIES SERIES

The *Iranian Studies Series* publishes high-quality scholarship on various aspects of Iranian civilisation, covering both contemporary and classical cultures of the Persian cultural area. The contemporary Persian-speaking area includes Iran, Afghanistan, Tajikistan, and Central Asia, while classical societies using Persian as a literary and cultural language were located in Anatolia, Caucasus, Central Asia and the Indo-Pakistani subcontinent. The objective of the series is to foster studies of the literary, historical, religious and linguistic products in Iranian languages. In addition to research monographs and reference works, the series publishes English-Persian critical text-editions of important texts. The series intends to publish resources and original research and make them accessible to a wide audience.

IRREVERENT PERSIA

INVECTIVE, SATIRICAL AND BURLESQUE POETRY FROM THE ORIGINS TO THE TIMURID PERIOD (10TH TO 15TH CENTURIES)

Riccardo Zipoli

Leiden University Press

Cover design: Tarek Atrissi Design
Cover illustration: Nizami's *Khamsa*. Shiraz, 1449–1450, New York, Metropolitan Museum of Art, 13.228.2, fol. 332r (Gift of Alexander Smith Cochran, 1913).
Lay-out: TAT Zetwerk, Utrecht

ISBN 978 90 8728 227 1
e-ISBN 978 94 0060 212 0 (ePDF)
e-ISBN 978 94 0060 213 7 (ePub)
NUR 635

This book is distributed in North America by the University of Chicago Press (www.press.uchicago.edu)

Contents

Notes on Transliteration System, Dates and Biographical Information

Except in cases for which there is a widely accepted spelling (such as Bukhara and Mu'âwiya), the Persian and Arabic terms have been transliterated following the rules proposed by the Library of Congress for Persian, but with no diacritical marks: only the long vowel 'a' is indicated as â (corresponding to a 'back' a). For the vowels and the diphthongs, the transliteration is based on the standard contemporary Persian pronunciation. The accent in Persian nouns falls on the last syllable.

Only the Christian era system of dates has been used with no corresponding Islamic dates. This rule does not apply to the year of publication for books cited in the bibliography, in which both dates are included (the Christian date first). When there is a double date for the Christian era (for example, 1160/1), this indicates that the corresponding year in the Islamic era straddles two years in the Christian era and it is not known in which of the two the event in question took place.

The poets' names are written in summarised form (in the Islamic world the name of a person often involves a long series of components), but in such a way as to make them easily identifiable. In cases of homonymy, an extra element is added, usually the *nisba* (indication of genealogical, ethnical or geographical provenance).

In an appendix at the end of the book there are brief biographical notes on the poets translated in the anthology. In the introduction all the names of people are accompanied by a reference date the first time they are mentioned.

There are no notes for well-known places or people (such as the prophet Muhammad) or unknown names (as happens, for example, with some persons contemporary to our poets). If a term requiring comment or explanation recurs several times in the same poem, the note appears at the first mention of the term.

The English equivalents of technical terms are provided only the first time that they occur, but a glossary of the key literary terms is provided at the end of the book.

Acknowledgements

I began this work in 1993 and, from the outset, I was lucky enough to rely on the invaluable collaboration of my friend and colleague Hamid Rezâ Bahârlu, who unfortunately died prematurely and whom I remember with deep and heart-felt gratitude. His help and intuitive insight were crucial in finding and interpreting the *corpus* collected here.

The work came into being at the prompting of Ehsan Yarshater, who also read through a preliminary version and offered advice. Encouragement and suggestions from François de Blois, Hans de Bruijn and Geert Jan van Gelder were of vital importance in completing the work. Lastly, it was due to the interest shown by Asghar Seyed-Gohrab that this book eventually found a prestigious publisher. I offer them all my warmest thanks.

Moreover, I should like to express my gratitude to Jalâl Moravvej and Gianroberto Scarcia for their extremely expert comments in the interpretation of controversial passages, and to Daniele Guizzo and Stefano Pellò who provided initial Italian translations of some of the texts. I am also deeply indebted to Gianroberto Scarcia, Daniela Meneghini, Daniele Guizzo and Stefano Pellò for reading and checking some parts of the book.

Finally, many thanks go to David Kerr for his essential contribution to drafting this text in English.

Introduction

The texts presented here come from a little studied area of Persian literature consisting of poems that reflect critical attitudes (ranging from gentle irony to elaborate condemnation and even crude verbal aggression) towards people, situations, aspects and products of social, political and cultural reality.

Our study deals with this kind of poetry from its origins (10th century) up to the Timurid period (15th century) and ends with the age of Jâmi (d. 1492), traditionally considered the last great classical Persian poet. Despite this relatively limited time scale, the field of inquiry is very rich. It embraces a broad range of literary genres that may be considered members of a single great typological family. These genres include invective, cursing, lampoon, satire, diatribe, mockery, facetiae, social criticism, burlesque, parody and the like. Some of them are so close in terms of intent, motivation, expression and content that they often overlap. Thus, it might be the case that a poem can be classified under more than one of these genres.

This raises a number of problems for anyone wishing to use the above labels in classifying the poems. Nonetheless, we believe that an approach based on these genres is useful in understanding and distinguishing the compositions we are dealing with. This approach can by itself give a useful idea of the structure of the entire corpus of the poetry in question.

A division according to the categories used in the Arabo-Persian tradition would not be so enlightening. According to that tradition, the texts referred to here are generally associated with two categories: *hajv/hejâ*[1] ('satire', 'mockery', 'verbal aggression') and *hazl* ('witticism', 'facetiae', 'bawdy poetry'). These two categories are so loose and wide-ranging that they are unsuitable for making a preliminary grouping of poems for the purposes of an overall classification and comprehension of the literary texts in question.

Some basic discussion of the structure and development of *hajv* and *hazl* in the Arabo-Persian tradition is, however, useful. Only in this way can we understand the original mechanisms and logic in our texts, making their links with the relevant Western literary genres clearer, and thus reducing the feeling that such genres are in some way being imposed from the outside.

The specific technical notions of *hajv* and *hazl* both came to the Persian world from Arabo-Islamic culture and preserved the original basic prerogatives of the respective models.[2] Like other literary phenomena adopted from the Arabo-Islamic tradition, once in the Persian context the *hajv* and *hazl* concepts assumed more of a functional and textual importance than a theoretical value, and critical reflection on the subject is rather rudimentary compared to the Arabic antecedents.[3]

The Genre of *Hajv* ('Satire', 'Mockery', 'Verbal Aggression')

The first *hajv* came into being in the pre-Islamic Arabic world as a kind of verbal weapon, with magic and defamatory power, used in tribal conflicts. Through *hajv*, the poet attacked, insulted and cursed his clan's enemies in order to humiliate them and undermine their position. With the advent of Islam, *hajv* continued to be practised in political and religious contexts but gradually began to lose some of its more militant force and was increasingly transformed from what was technically a political instrument into a complex literary phenomenon. It lost none of its offensive characteristics and became the main instrument for expressing criticism, censure and condemnation. At the same time *hajv* acquired a vast range of contents and accents (moralistic along with, for example, obscene and witty tones), which provided a more elaborate literary theme or genre (*gharaz*) compared to the other, more homogeneous, traditional themes or genres in classical Arabic poetry such as *marsiyye* (elegy), *madih* (panegyric),[4] *nasib*/ghazal (lyric) and *fakhr* (self-praise). It was not unusual, however, for Arab theorists to describe *hajv* reductively as simply the opposite of *madih*.

Having entered the Persian literary world, *hajv* preserved its own dignity and importance on a par with other poetic genres, as Key Kâ'us (d. 1098) points out:

> Whatever form your poetry has, *madh*, ghazal, *hejâ*, *marsiyye* or *zohd* (poetry of abstinence), write it in the most appropriate way possible and never express anything in a manner that may be considered imperfect.[5]

In Persian, *hajv* preserved most of the functional features connoting it in the Arabic world. It is thus primarily seen as a powerful verbal weapon capable of dishonouring and ruining the *mahju* (victim of satire). This conviction was present in various ancient texts. The author of the *Târikh-e Beyhaqi* (11th century), for example, describing the power struggle after the death of the caliph Hârun ar-Rashid,[6] says of the Grand Vizier Fazl ebn-e Rabiʿ:

> Fazl ordered that Ma'mun be stripped of the title of crown prince and he told the preachers to offend him from the pulpit and commanded the poets to write *hejâ* about him.[7]

Shams-e Qeys (fl. first half of the 13th century), on the other hand, warned against antagonising poets to avoid their taking revenge by impugning people's honour. This recommendation originated from first-hand experience. Having unwittingly offended a poetaster, Shams-e Qeys became a target for the poetaster's *hajv* and so wrote:

> Thanks to the advice that I gave him out of courtesy, people will read *hajv* and insults about me from Khorasan to Iraq.[8]

One famous episode is narrated by Nezâmi-ye ʿAruzi (12th century) about Ferdowsi (d. 1019 or 1025) and the *hajv* that he wrote to shame the Ghaznavid sultan Mahmud (r. 998–1030), guilty of having treated him badly.[9] In this *hajv* Ferdowsi himself stresses the lasting effect of *hajv*:

> The poet, if angered, will write *hejâ*,
> and that *hejâ* will last till Judgment Day.[10]

Many poems underscore this effect of *hajv*. Among the earliest examples is the following poem, which Shams-e Qeys quotes and attributes to Mo'ayyadi (12th century):

> Not everyone knows how to put prose into poetry,
> poetic skill is a gift from the incomparable Protector.
>
> So if a poet likes to boast, do not be surprised:
> he was lucky to receive this privilege from God!
>
> His *madih* lifts people up to the Great Bear,
> with his *hejâ* he covers heads with ashes.

A thought may also go well in prose, but it improves
if a poet turns it into verse with fine expressions.

Poetry makes the cheerful happy on feast days,
and fills soldiers with pride on the eve of battle.

But if a poet leaves his brand on a person,
the person will never be able to get rid of it.

Try therefore, as far as you can, to keep poets satisfied,
if you are wise and intelligent, you won't annoy them.[11]

A similar but more elaborate comment is provided by Rumi (d. 1273):

If your panegyrist makes *hajv* on you in public,
your heart will smart for days from the scathing.

Although you know that he said all those words
disappointed at having lost the hopes he had in you,

their effect will linger deep inside.
Something similar is felt with *madih*,

because its effect will also last for some time.
But you become proud and your soul is deceived,

without you realizing it, because the *madh* is sweet,
whereas with *hajv* you feel the bitter pain of accusation:

it is as bitter as a decoction or pill you have to swallow,
leaving you upset and suffering for days and days on end.

This is not so when you taste sweet halva: the flavour lingers,
but only for a while, as its effect is transitory and vanishes.[12]

Significantly, *hajv* is often described in Persian poetry as a real weapon (a spear, for example, or a sword) or as a kind of makeshift (a penis or a laxative) for the purpose, in both cases, of meting out an exemplary punishment. Here are two lines by Shatranji (12th century), alluding to the two functions:

Your deceitful promises grow fast and thick,
O hypocrite dog, and, through this behaviour,

I fear you want me to stick some lines of *hejâ* up your wife's arse,
just as spears are run through pagan heads, ready to be paraded.[13]

And, indeed, as if it were a weapon, the use of *hajv* is sometimes threatened as the last resort. Here is an example from Anvari (d. c. 1186):

I've addressed you *madh* as immaculate as a virgin cunt,
I've burst through the arse of my mind with great passion,

but now if you don't fuck me with the cock of a gift,
I'll squeeze the balls of *hajv* against you from behind.[14]

Kamâl od-Din (d. 1237) makes a very significant remark on this point. He suggests that skill in writing *hajv* must be an integral part of the repertoire of any poet:

Although writing *hejâ* is not agreeable,
God forbid a poet to be unpractised in it.

The poet who knows nothing of *hejâ*,
is like a lion with no claws or teeth.

If you don't study how to write *hejâ* from the start,
it's as if you had never been to school in this world.[15]

Some reports about the inconsolable reactions caused by *hajv* confirm its power to offend, as in the following line by Labibi (fl. first half of the 11th century):

When you eventually sit down and read this *hejâ* with care,
you'll tear out your beard, your wife the hairs from her pubes.[16]

All of this involves obvious dangers for the poets. There are thus invitations to use this harmful instrument sparingly, such as Key Kâ'us's warning:

Don't get into the habit of writing *hejâ*, since doughnuts don't always come out with a hole.[17]

On the other hand, some poets vaunted the fact that they never indulged in this instrumental use of poetry. ʿAbd ol-Vâseʿ-e Jabali (d. 1160), for example, asserts:

> For me this is a great boast: no one can claim to have seen
> an accusation in my prose and a line of *hejâ* in my poetry.[18]

But often these are purely rhetorical claims, as in the case of Khâqâni (d. c. 1199), whose output of *hajv* is in fact considerable:

> In my poems you will never come across a single line of *hajv*,
> just as in the garden of paradise you won't find a single thorn.[19]

Such a denial is part of a conventional use of disavowals, characterising especially the more outrageous examples of *hajv* poetry. Obviously, it was not advisable to express official approval of this kind of poetry openly.[20]

In addition to being a verbal weapon, *hajv* is seen in the Persian world, in line with the Arabic tradition, as the opposite of *madh*. Again, Key Kâ'us is eloquent on the subject:

> If you want to write *hejâ* and don't feel up to it, say the exact opposite of what you would say to the same person in writing *madh*, because *hejâ* is its opposite, just as ghazal is the opposite of *marsiyye*.[21]

Sometimes the poets themselves also set *hajv* and *madh* as antithetical terms. The difference between the respective effects on the addressee has already been evidenced in the passage attributed to Mo'ayyadi and that by Rumi, but the two phenomena are often opposed in relation to the poet himself. There are many examples, such as this line by Manuchehri (d. c. 1040):

> The time has now come to do without *hejâ* and *madih*:
> *hejâ* has harmed me and I've had no benefits from *madih*.[22]

At times the antithesis concerns both the personality of the poet and the consequences for the addressee, as Jamâl od-Din (fl. second half of the 12th century) reminds us:

> When composing *madh*, I am like the sun spreading light,
> when composing *hajv*, I am like the sky destroying men:
>
> my *madh* words convey nectar full of honey,
> my pen writing *hajv* is a snake spitting venom.[23]

Of modern critics, Bertel's gives one of the clearest descriptions of this antithesis:

> The satire (*hajv*) of this period [10th century] takes us into a completely different atmosphere of artistic creation. While in the panegyric and similar forms all the poet's efforts are bent towards an idealization of the person praised and surrounding that person with a halo, satire has the diametrically opposite function: that of breaking the halo and making the defamed person appear in ridiculous or repugnant guises. Accordingly, the vocabulary changes because the poet, in describing filth, slovenliness and physical defects and deformities, naturally has to resort to words unacceptable in high literature. Particularly interesting is the fact that in satires we even occasionally find regional expressions, extraneous to literary language and thus highlighting how near these works are to the spoken language of the time. Nonetheless, these satires must not be considered as realistic works. The poetry that has reached us evokes grotesque caricatures which have nothing to do with realism. Rivals are represented as abominable, repugnant scarecrows in whose beards spiders weave their webs. Exaggeration is taken to extremes and it is impossible to reconstruct any kind of realistic picture from a series of insults. Indeed, in satire there is a parallel idealization of what is found in the panegyric but oriented, so to speak, in the opposite direction: it stresses everything that the panegyric scrupulously passes over in silence.[24]

Notwithstanding comments and reflections of this kind, Persian *hajv*, like its Arabic antecedent, cannot simply be defined as the negative of the *madh*. It is a very elaborate literary phenomenon that includes not only satire (the term most widely used today to provide a translation) but, in different ways and guises, also many of the other 'sister' genres we listed at the beginning. Despite this complexity, a *hajv* text can be easily identified as such because of a number of well-defined features.

Firstly, let us look at the most common type of *hajv*. In this first type, the texts, in addition to a strong and structural critical approach, have humorous elements. They may make use of crude, direct images, at times obscene, also characterised by colloquial vocabulary and hyperbolic fantasies. Some of these tendencies, especially the obscene and colloquial, obviously violate the classical code. The overall structure of this code, however, not only with regard to rhetoric and prosody but also in terms of vocabulary and images, is preserved in the texts, thus ensuring the continuity of tradition. The coexistence and combination of classical and innovative elements is one of the typical and striking features of this type of *hajv* and it permeates various aspects of it. For example, the usual figures of speech (especially similes, metaphors, hyperboles, 'fantastic etiologies', personifications and semantic analogies) are often dissociated from the usual models, which remain in the background as memory, and are applied in provocative and shocking ways to new subjects and contexts. This all produces a series of contrasts which, to be fully understood and enjoyed, requires deep knowledge of and comparison with the traditional canons. Each aspect of the stylistic heritage is called into question, starting from the pen-name. Thus we find a poet using the irreverent pen-name Kir-e Khar ('Donkey's Cock') in Râduyâni's *Tarjomân ol-Balâghe* (late 11th century).[25] The effect is desecrating and aims not only to capture the readers' attention but also to make them smile. Amir Khosrow (d. 1325) offers some enlightening remarks on the subject:

> Regarding the apparently vain vaunt and ostentatious display of glory when I described the camel's dung as the choicest perfume of civet cat (or the best cream of its milk), it was nothing but a facetious expression of pleasantry that I offered to the well-directed ones for mirth and amusement. When what was a mere 'Darmana' grass or hyssop was given the name of powdered saffron, my object was to step up laughter at the expense of the merits of my own poetical pieces.[26]

In the dialectic between the old and the new a key function is played by the themes, whose novelty brings shocking comic elements to the existing repertoire. In the general context of personal topics, the most disturbing elements concern the disparaging of important symbols in the Islamic tradition, such as the beard or male organ, and the violation of basic taboos related to cleanliness, nudity, sexual activities and the family. The descriptions are often amusing caricatures highlighting instincts and animal needs (eating, drinking, defecating, vomiting, having sex, etc.) in the attempt to humiliate rivals and bring them into disrepute. This kind of facetious and outrageous *hajv* is the most typical and widely found.

There is also, however, a variant of *hajv* with serious tones and content, more in line with tradition. Although less significant and representative of *hajv* in the overall sense, this variant is generally more appreciated by the critics, compared to its facetious and outrageous counterpart: its moderate approach makes it morally and aesthetically acceptable. Frank humour is replaced by irony, crudity is stripped of obscenity, fantasy no longer reaches extreme heights, the vocabulary and imagery remain within the classical canon, the subjects no longer have outrageous accents and here concern, above all, ethical and intellectual faults such as avarice, corruption and pride. A conscientious point of view takes over from material calculations and individual interests: the poet prefers to stigmatise and denounce the *mahju* rather than make him the butt of humiliation and ridicule.

Many factors condition a poet in choosing which of the two variants of *hajv*, facetious or serious, to use. The causes inspiring it, its purposes and the types of *mahju* are certainly very important.

Various causes may drive the poet to compose *hajv*. They are often identified and described by the poet himself: he may be rebelling against an insult or a wrong done to him or his patron; he may be involved in a dispute with another poet; he may be disappointed at not having received hoped-for gifts, possibly promised by the patron; or he may be reacting to private or public customs and behaviour that he views as questionable. Other more unfathomable reasons may be related to existential dissatisfaction and could derive, for example, from psychological complexes or physical problems.

As with the causes, the purposes of these poems are also often identified and described by the poet himself. Summarising what we have said so far, the main purpose of these compositions is to attack and denounce individuals or groups of individuals that the poet deems to be his rivals or his patron's enemies. Sometimes the personal vein is diluted and the poet is concerned to highlight vices and defects of a moral, political or social nature, and, in such circumstances, may even suggest remedies and solutions. The purpose is literary when the poet focuses on phenomena limited to the art of writing. In the frequent cases in which the poet is a court professional, he obviously also aims to entertain his patron and entourage and to obtain some recompense.

The type of *mahju* is also crucial. There are various types of *mahju* and their status obviously influences the tone of the composition. In most cases the target is an individual, whose name may or may not be mentioned and whose position as part of a socio-political category is generally established (sovereign, poet, minister, judge, family member, acquaintance, enemy and the like). The *mahju* may also be a group or class of people and can be identified collectively: for example, as a particular religious order, the inhabitants of a city, a professional category or a set of people sharing the same attitudes. Lastly, the poet may fire his criticism, not at people and human contexts, but at literary phenomena: the *mahju* in this case may be a genre, form, style, type of lexicon or something similar.

Whatever its characteristics, *hajv* poetry, like any other poetic expression in that literary world, must observe a set of conventional rules in order to guarantee its own plausibility and enjoyment as a literary product. In other words, as we have said above, it must show those linguistic, rhetorical and prosodic expedients typical of Persian poetry in general. Consequently, the content of *hajv*, as with all kinds of Persian poetry, is a subject that the poet must above all be concerned to dress in beautiful and polished forms. In this case too, judging the merits of a poem in a traditional way means focusing more on the effectiveness of the *elocutio* than the materials of the *inventio*, which basically remain the same throughout the centuries.

This formal attitude suggests a key for interpreting *hajv* compositions, whereby the aesthetic-intellectual aspects are more important than the socio-political and emotional circumstances. From this point of view, the text becomes a kind of verbal performance in which what is displayed and tested is the poet's compositional skill rather than his personal feelings and reactions. Indeed, the themes are actually often so conventional and predictable that they can be considered part of the related poetic code. The *extra-text*, in other words, appears in many cases to be of little relevance for the purposes of a textual evaluation, and simply takes on the features of a *pre-text* for what is mainly a display of artistry. In this situation, the rhetorical function of the poem assumes a greater role compared to the criticism conveyed, and contrivance overshadows the sincerity of the inspiration. The text thus adopts the tones of a literary act that may be enjoyed beyond the related socio-political and emotional context. This kind of interpretation is in line with the general canons of the Persian poetic tradition, in which the panegyric vein shares similar formal inspiration.

There are, however, some situations in which the content of *hajv*, again analogous in this sense to panegyrical poetry, is crucial and the focus of attention. Here the knowledge of personal and political circumstances is fundamental to understanding the passages in question. But such circumstances may be difficult to grasp or even wholly incomprehensible today, limiting, or even preventing not only the interpretation but also the enjoyment of such texts. These may well be *hajv* poems that were very successful in their day, but since their interpretative key has been lost they are much more difficult to appreciate today. In such cases the socio-political and emotional circumstances overshadow the aesthetic-intellectual aspects.

In line with these distinctions, the relationship between a poet and his audience may also vary. To cite two extreme possibilities, it may range from a technical understanding, involving the encoding and decoding of texts, to a kind of psychological complicity fuelled by the sense of superiority towards the denounced subjects and pleasure in the effrontery and transgression.

The Genre of *Hazl* ('Witticism', 'Facetiae', 'Bawdy Poetry')

Just as the term *hajv* is set in opposition to *madh*, *hazl*, again following the Arabic tradition, is opposed to *jedd* (earnestness) in the Persian world. This antithesis is documented in old texts, such as the *Târikh-e Beyhaqi*:

> Your speech is *jedd*, not spiteful joys and *hazl*.[27]

There are numerous poems on this topic. An example is the following lines by Manuchehri about 'Onsori (d. 1039), where the *hazl/jedd* pair, accompanied by the *hajv/madh* pair, seems to indicate the complete range of possible behaviour as a writer:

> He is calm like a mountain with a cave of peace,
> his nature is like a sea with the pearls of the mind:
>
> in his poetry and in his prose, in his *madh* and in his *hajv*,
> in his *jedd* and his *hazl*, when he writes and when he drinks.[28]

As in the case of *hajv*, the boundaries of *hazl* are rather wide-ranging and loose. It actually shares the same expressive features as the most typical *hajv*, being witty, often crudely direct and striking in its fantastic and outrageous invention as well as in its blending of classical and innovative vocabulary and imagery. *Hazl* shares with *hajv* the same addressees and the same audience, but its emphasis on amusement is more significant than the critical intent. In *hazl* no judgement or serious commitment is necessarily expressed. It reflects a playful and frivolous attitude and focuses on the comic and nonsensical side of human affairs leaving aside political or social discontent and denunciation. In this sense *hazl* is less anchored to reality than *hajv*, and is distinguished by a greater freedom in distorting contents and references. Among its specific official tasks is that of entertaining by distracting and attracting the public at the same time, following some specific lines of the *adab* literature.[29] Its most typical feature is obscenity, often leading it to be identified, in the view of Persian authors, with humorously bawdy anecdotes.

The situation is not, however, always unequivocal and clear-cut. Sometimes poems, although amusing and daring in the *hazl* sense we have just described, also express political or social discontent and denunciation, rightfully taking their place among the texts we wish to present in this book. The borderline between *hazl* and *hajv* is a very grey area in this case, as has been evidenced by some critics who deal with them as two branches, one comic and the other serious, of the same 'tree'.[30] In fact, compositions technically defined as *hazl* may reveal an alternation or a mixture of the typical tones of *hazl* (generally condemned as anti-ethical) and critical accents associated with a more responsible, sometimes even morally impeccable, involvement. This often led to contradictory attitudes on the part of Persian authors towards the phenomenon of *hazl*. The differences in judgement depend on the various contexts and purposes of the output in question. There are, thus, expressions of disapproval, as in these lines by Nâser-e Khosrow (d. c. 1077) where the opposition between *hazl* and *jedd* is stressed:

Don't make lies, swearing and *hazl* your trade:
don't go and cut off your nose to spite your face!

If you lie, when judged fairly,
you do not have a bright future.

He who swears when speaking,
won't be respected and esteemed.

Anyone practising *hazl* will certainly lose all his honour,
even if a king, and will be humiliated, even if the moon:

instinct leads to *hazl* and enjoys it,
but the mind seeks and delights in *jedd*.

Arguments that set out to honour wisdom
must be stripped of lies, swearing and *hazl*.

The soul will be dowsed if you engage in *hazl* every day,
but a radiant instinct becomes like the spirit through *jedd*.[31]

Disapproval of *hazl* is also expressed at times by authors, such as Monjik (fl. second half of the 10th century), who are notorious for their outrageous passages.[32] This highlights differences in judgement even within works by the same author:

> I won't listen to absurdities, lies or *hazl*:
> saying *hazl* is always heresy in Islam.[33]

Sanâ'i and Rumi, who, as we shall see below, support the didactic usefulness of *hazl*, also express a similar negative opinion, generally discouraging and condemning *hazl*. Sanâ'i claims:

> Every time a judicious person hears *hazl*,
> he plugs his ears with the fingers of religion.
>
> When a frivolous spirit spouts *hazl*,
> people will rightly grow hard of hearing.[34]

And Rumi says:

> Close the bodily eyes to *hazl* and lies,
> and you'll see the city of the bright soul.[35]

Sharing these negative opinions, Owhadi (d. 1338) gives a clear warning of the dangers involved in writing *hazl*:

> *Hazl* can bring shame on you,
> and, if excessive, also enemies.[36]

Criticism of *hazl* poetry may even be accompanied—in a rather unusual combination—by negative comments on *madh* verse. In the following line by ʿAttâr (d. 1221) it is the general human and social context, whether praised or mocked, which is called into question for the purposes of a philosophical-type reflection.

> Composing verse with *madh* or *hazl* tones is tantamount to nothing,
> it is better to write poetry on wisdom since it has no twisted logic.[37]

In addition to these severe judgements, however, we find a number of positive opinions about *hazl*. The utilitarian interpretations of *hazl*, proffered in the collection of fables entitled *Kalile o Demne* (completed c. 1144), are a good example:

> The chapters of the book are based on wisdom and spiritual warnings in a setting, however, of *hazl*, so that ordinary people, thanks to this *hazl*, will be induced to read it and gradually become familiar with its truths, in the same way that high-ranking people are normally attracted to this book to gain experience.[38]

Positive judgments on *hazl* are expressed especially in relation to its opposite *jedd*, as in this line by Anvari:

> Only wiseacres are devoted to *jedd* without ever indulging in *hazl*:
> this kind of speech anguishes the soul and makes boredom grow.[39]

We are generally talking, in any case, about a measured use of *hazl*, the function of which is often compared to that of salt in food, as Sanâ'i claims:

> *Jedd* expressions with no *hazl* are bland,
> food requires salt to be truly savoury.[40]

A famous example of this approach is the opening of the *Resâle-ye Delgoshâ* by 'Obeyd (d. c. 1370):

> The faculty of speech, on which depends the nobility of man, has two aspects, *jedd* and *hazl*. Although *jedd* is undoubtedly superior to *hazl*, when *jedd is* continuous, it brings boredom, just as uninterrupted *hazl* leads to disdain and disrepute. On this subject the ancients have said:
>
> > All year *jedd* wears out the soul,
> > all day *hazl* ruins your honour.
>
> Having said this, to dispel boredom and cheer up the spirit, refined people have at times been interested in a certain kind of *hazl*, in keeping with the saying of the wise, whereby '*hazl* must be used in words, like salt in food', which is the same invitation that can be read in the following lines:
>
> > Relieve your troubled tormented mind
> > with pleasant sayings and witticisms,
> >
> > but don't use them overmuch;
> > dose them well, like salt in food.

The poet's thought is thus enacted when he says:

> Even when talking about the unique God and about eloquence
> you can indulge in nonsense, but only gracefully and moderately.

All of this will be forgiven, since our great considered it licit![41]

This attitude of moderate approval also affects the contents of *hazl*, as can be seen in the following lines by Jâmi:

> The garden is joyous with smiling flowers,
> a smile is indeed fitting dress for the wise.
>
> Smiling is certainly different from *jedd*,
> but continuous *jedd* is not indispensable.
>
> The heart suffers because of *jedd* from morning
> to evening: cheer up your spirits with *hazl*!
>
> *Jedd* is like hurting your feet on a unending walk,
> *hazl* is like a moment of relief along that road.
>
> If the relief fails to soothe the wound,
> you will surely perish from the pain.
>
> But *hazl* must not end up darkening
> the bright face of your *jedd* with lies,
>
> and thus sow the seeds of rancour in hearts,
> making the brow bead with shame's sweat.
>
> Be inspired, therefore, by enlightening wisdom,
> and say just things, but in a sweet witticism![42]

As we have seen, the positive attitude to *hazl* focuses on the use of light and pleasant poetry without any reference to its outrageous and obscene variant. It must be said, however, that even those who argue that elegant, moderate *hazl* is the only acceptable form often indulge in poetry with decidedly indecent tones, thus evidencing the widespread dichotomy in that world between the theory and practice of writing poetry.

In the context of the *hazl/jedd* pair, it is also significant that the great masters of mysticism acknowledged the didactic usefulness of *hazl*. This is what Sanâ'i says on the subject:

Jedd has clearly nothing at all to do with *hazl*,
but my *hazl* poetry and my *jedd* poetry are kin:

in the treasure honouring the sovereign,
both beautiful and ugly things can be seen.

My *hazl* is not simple *hazl*, it is instruction!
My poems are not simply poems, but a universe!

And do you know how the master's mind
exercises his teaching in that universe?

While his *jedd* cheers up the listener,
his *hazl*, with its magic, inspires the soul.

I thank God that, for experienced people,
my *hazl* is more welcome than others' *jedd*.[43]

Rumi literally borrows (albeit with the hemistichs inverted) the third line by Sanâ'i just quoted,[44] and also repeats this opinion in greater detail:

Hazl is instruction: consider it equal to *jedd*,
don't be deceived by its appearance as *hazl*!

Every *jedd* is *hazl* for a *hazl* person,
every *hazl* is *jedd* for a *jedd* person.[45]

The great master of the art of life, Sa'di, is of a similar opinion:

I didn't say these things for pure amusement,
leave their *hazl* side and look to their *jedd*![46]

An expert like 'Obeyd is more categorical and explicit in his *Resâle-ye Sad Pand*:

Don't despise *hazl* and don't disdain whoever writes it![47]

To complete this assessment of *hazl*, we would like to quote some other comments justifying the presence of such expressions only in specific circumstances. Here is the advice given by Key Kâ'us to his son:

> Jesting may be tolerated but offence should never be given. If you cannot resist making crude quips and unworthy gestures, make sure they are not aimed at people below your social rank, because you would expose your dignity to the ignominy of their reaction. Choose your peers and, if they reply, then no ill will come of it. Ensure that your *hazl* is, in any case, alternated with *jedd* and do not go so far as to be insulting. Although jesting inevitably involves some *hazl*, be careful not to overstep the mark, because you will be in danger of cutting a petty figure.[48]

The same balanced approach is advocated by Key Kâ'us when addressing an ideal boon companion for the sovereign:

> He must be dedicated to both *jedd* and *hazl*, showing an awareness of the appropriate moment for each by not saying *hazl* when the moment requires *jedd* and not showing *jedd* when everyone is saying *hazl*.[49]

Again on the subject of the relation between *hazl* and the sovereign's boon companions, Nezâm ol-Molk (d. 1092) claims:

> The sovereign can say a thousand different things, both *jedd* and *hazl*, to his boon companions, things that he could never say to his minister and other dignitaries ... Only with his boon companions can he be completely at ease. With them he spends carefree moments, and tells witty curious stories and even pleasantries mixed with *hazl*, without his honour or regal nature being impaired. He has them with him precisely for this reason.[50]

In line with this measured approach is what Shams-e Qeys notes on the subject, even if he does not actually mention the word *hazl*:

> Human speech is as varied and different as the kinds and classes of people. Speech can be beautiful and ugly, good and bad, pleasant and weak, and all these forms are widespread and often practised. And it may be the case that unpleasant witticisms and silly quips are well suited also to important gatherings and bring greater success than pleasant witticisms and subtle quips to those who pronounce them on such occasions. The same happens with the catamite ballads. Despite their vulgar expressions and base content, they manage in some gatherings to give pleasure that goes beyond that generated by more admirable words and elegant poems.

> Given this situation, rejecting some statements and rebuking someone for what they say is neither perceptive nor wise, and is against the rules of virtuous people.[51]

This series of comments highlights how the approach to *hazl* is more elaborate and complex than that to *hajv*. In fact *hajv* and *hazl* are usually dealt with and described as two different categories but, as we have already suggested, *hajv* poetry and the *hazl* poetry expressing political or social criticism (i.e. the two kinds of poems making up the corpus of our book) are ultimately so close that, in terms of their historical development in the Persian world, they may be considered two sub-divisions, each with its own specific characteristics, of a single category.

Historical Background

Significantly, two of the earliest examples of Persian poetry (not yet influenced by Arabic prosody) show precisely those features of invective and satirical poetry typical of the majority of our corpus. The first example, containing touches of *hajv* and *hazl*, was composed towards the end of the 7th century by Ebn-e Mofarregh (d. 688). Guilty of having written *hajv* against his lord, the poet was punished: having been surreptitiously administered a laxative, he was left in the streets of Basra tied to some animals, including a pig. When the laxative took effect and some stinking liquid began to drip on the pig from the poet's clothes, some boys in the street asked him what it was, to which he replied:

> It is water, date juice,
> with nectar of dried figs,
> and the pig is Somayye.[52]

Somayye was the mother of Ebn-e Mofarregh's lord. Interestingly, the poet was of Arab stock, and this fact seems symbolically to mark the entry of this specific Arabic tradition into the Persian world.[53]

The second example is a set of *hajv* lines recited at Balkh by a group of boys poking fun at Asad ebn-e 'Abdollâh (d. 738) when he returned in 726 after being defeated in a campaign against the lord of Khatlân:

> You are back from Khatlân,
> you are back in disgrace,
> you are back in disarray,
> you are back scraggy and skinny![54]

The interesting feature in this second example is its popular aspect, suggesting that this kind of poetic attitude had autochthonous Persian roots, onto which the inheritance from the Arabic world was grafted.[55] On closer examination, it truly seems to have been a successful combination: Arabic culture provided the Persian world with a complex heritage of technical forms and content concerning *hajv* and *hazl*, and the Persians, for their part, found this specific inheritance so congenial that they soon made it a lively part of their new literary tradition.

And in fact the development of *hajv* and *hazl* poetry in Persian follows the development and fate of all Persian poetry. The first significant examples date from the Samanid period (10th century) and testify in general to disputes of poets with rival poets, with their patrons and with other, not always identifiable, figures. Here is what Bertel's has to say on the subject:

> A characteristic feature of the poetry of that time [10th century] was the development of satire (*hajv*). To be precise the use of the word satire is not completely appropriate here. In fact 10th-century *hajv* is not what we usually mean by satire. In similar poetic compositions there is no kind of social criticism (any criticism of the ruling class was even unthinkable). The purpose of these satires was in general only to eliminate rivals. The authors mainly poured scorn on their rivals and accused them of the most disgusting vices, even resorting to false accusations without the least scruple. The less talent a poet had, the more he concentrated on satire, thus trying to carve out a successful career. At that time satire was typically considered unworthy of respectable people and it was usually not included in collections of poems. Only individual fragments of these satires have survived. But this is no great loss. These compositions are interesting only from the linguistic point of view: unlike panegyrics, they are written in a humble style, and for this reason may contain some very interesting vocabulary.[56]

This ethical and aesthetic judgement by Bertel's appears to be unjustly severe. In the light of our readings, we must also revise the notion that the ruling class was above criticism, although freedom of speech is more evident after the 10th century. On the other hand, there can be no doubt about the linguistic importance of these poems, despite the fact that they have only survived in isolated lines and are often difficult to interpret.

A major source at the linguistic level in this context is the *Loghat-e Fors* (10th century), the earliest Persian monolingual dictionary to have survived in several manuscripts. It contains many lines of *hajv* and *hazl*. Significantly, a number of obscene lines are used to illustrate entry words which are not obscene. The presence of such lines is thus due to the choice made by the lexicographer, who could easily have selected illustrative lines of a different kind.[57] This may suggest that the lines in question were particularly useful for the purposes of exemplification, probably because they were well known.

Regarding their textual features (especially the lexicon and imagery), the 10th-century examples are fairly far removed from the complex, daring compositions of later periods. This is both because of their brevity and because they are part of the as yet not fully-developed origins of Persian poetry itself. The many authors include ʿAmmâre, Maʿrufi, Monjik and Shahid.

In the Ghaznavid period, parallel to the rise of the first great panegyrists in the 11th century, there was a considerable development in the output of *hajv/hazl*, with the first long poems in this mode. A typically prolific author was Labibi, but some traditionally more celebrated poets also wrote *hajv*: Ferdowsi lashed out at the Ghaznavid sovereign Mahmud;[58] Manuchehri rebuked a rival who envied him at court;[59] while ʿOnsori clashed with Ghazâʾeri, giving rise to one of the earliest disputes in Persian poetry.[60]

At the end of the 11th and beginning of the 12th centuries, with Sanâʾi we find the first substantial examples of *hajv/hazl* focused not only on personal matters (the dominant trend at the time to which the same Sanâʾi had contributed through many poems) but also extended to wider-ranging issues with social and political hues. It was also Sanâʾi, in his role as writer of both religious texts and *hazl*, who paved the way for the use of *hazl* in mystical poetry. From then on, *hazl* elements, like all the other elements from the earlier secular heritage, were enlisted in spreading the spiritual message, as was well exemplified a century later by a good deal of Rumi's poetry.

Like panegyric, this poetry took off in the Saljuq period: in the 12th century *hajv* and *hazl* often became so thoroughly mixed as to be inextricable in many cases. One of the most striking features of this output is great inventive skill, reflecting analogous developments in contemporary serious poetry.

This flourishing of *hajv* and *hazl* was encouraged by the difficult socio-political situation that generated more occasions for disputes between poets and also between poets and patrons. It is unusual to find a 12th-century poet who has not composed some lines of *hajv* and *hazl*, but the prize, both for quantity and quality, is usually awarded to Suzani and Anvari. For his part, Khâqâni is often classed as one of the touchiest and most irascible poets. The targets of his poetry include his master Abu 'l-ʿAlâ', his supposed pupil Mojir od-Din, some contemporary poets such as Vatvât, masters of the past (ʿOnsori) and his own family (his father). Among the other significant poets in this period were ʿAmʿaq, Asir od-Din-e Akhsikati, Jamâl od-Din, Mojir od-Din, Mokhtâri, Qamar, Ruhi, Shatranji and Zahir od-Din-e Fâryâbi. Kamâl od-Din and Qomri were trenchant and prolific poets at the end of the 12th and the beginning of the 13th centuries.

In the 13th century, Saʿdi considerably furthered the tradition of this kind of poetry with his ironic and amused comments on the vicissitudes of daily life. Although very audacious *hazl* poetry has been attributed to him, most of his *hajv* is in a sincere and moralizing style that was further elaborated in the 14th century by Hâfez, Khâju and, especially, ʿObeyd, whose acute observations of the social and political scene opened a new chapter in the history of this kind of poetry. Two other 14th-century poets with a watchful critical eye on public life were Ebn-e Yamin and Owhadi.

With the advent of the Timurid dynasty in the 15th century, the output of *hajv/hazl* again shared the fate of all contemporary poetry: it spread endemically among the various strata of the population, and at times reached extremely refined heights, as can be seen in the poetry of Boshâq, Qâri and Jâmi, who marks the chronological limit of our survey.[61]

Poetic Forms

The range of poetic forms used in *hajv/hazl* poetry is broad. The *qetʿe* is the most recurrent form, thanks mainly to its nature, which permits freedom in choosing themes even from the sphere of daily life, and its formal flexibility. In this form, the rhyme in the initial hemistich is usually omitted and the number of lines may vary. The *qaside*, commonly used for panegyric, that is, the opposite of *hajv*, can also be used for *hajv/hazl* (this is also attested to in the Arabic tradition). *Masnavi* (long poems with rhyming couplets) and *robâʿi* (quatrains) are both well suited to composing *hajv/hazl*, albeit for different reasons. Because of its length and its rhyming scheme with a different rhyme in every line, which are elements making it easier to develop the narrative, the *masnavi* is an ideal vehicle for two common forms of *hajv/hazl*: monologues and stories.[62] The *robâ'i*, on the other hand, because of its brevity, is an epigrammatic form particularly suitable for hitting the mark pithily and for memorising. The ghazal is not frequently used in composing *hajv/hazl*. Its identification with the lyric and its extremely rigid codification leave little room for the kind of inspiration found in the bold ideas of *hajv/hazl*. Its use in this context is generally limited to 'serious' satire aimed at bigotry and hypocrisy. Moreover, the ghazal tends to present a different theme or idea in each line and the consequent semantic independence of individual lines is not suited to the mainly narrative structure typical of poems dealing with *hajv/hazl*. If this kind of poetry appears in a ghazal, however, it seldom indulges in crude and overly-brazen tones. Exceptions are two famous *tarji'band* (strophic poems) whose stanzas are, in fact, each made up of a sort of ghazal with *hajv/hazl* contents.[63] The overall structure of the *tarji'band* may indeed be considered less lyrically fragmented thanks to the refrain after each stanza, allowing a certain thematic continuity to be maintained.

Tradition of Studies

Despite the wide-ranging and rich picture of *hajv/hazl* in Persian literature, the tradition of studies on the subject is very scanty. This reflects a generally accepted traditional view also in other literary worlds whereby poetry of censure or criticism in general—not just because of its content but also due to its vague broad boundaries—is usually considered a kind of illegitimate sister compared to genres codified in a more well-defined and clear fashion. Moreover, our studies even run into hostility when dealing with those texts that have an outrageous vocabulary and imagery. The obscenity typical of many of our texts is so embarrassing for scholars as to inhibit activity at all levels (critical editions, textual analyses, historical studies, theorisation) and research has suffered as a result.[64] In these cases, we are faced not simply with a lack of interest but also a prejudice, generated in particular by the fear of those very taboos that our poets delighted in violating.[65] The damage to a deeper understanding of the whole of Persian literary history is self-evident. It would be like claiming to write and study the history of Latin literature while neglecting the cruder sections of the satires of Martial and

Juvenal.[66] Here we wish to try and reverse this trend. Our aims include the possibility for readers to become familiar with some of the pages neglected in traditional studies, i.e. some outrageous sections of *hajv* and *hazl* poetry. Such a contribution is important not only from the historical, literary and aesthetic points of view, but also because this kind of poetry is notably representative of the culture at the centre of our interests, bearing in mind the great popularity it enjoyed and still enjoys with Iranian readers, as one eminent scholar points out:

> Facetious poetry's success and popularity are mainly due to ordinary people's interest in futile insults and trenchant witticisms. It is precisely because of this that authors of *hazl* such as Monjik of Termez, Tayyân-e Zhâzhkhây [10th century], Suzani of Samarkand, Hakim Kushkaki [12th century], Yaghmâ [d. 1859] and Iraj [d. 1926] have become renowned and their poetry has spread among ordinary people more or less to the same extent as ballads and popular songs. Their trenchant witticisms met with favour because they afford that pleasure which many take in seeing others as the target of humiliation and moral rebuke, especially if accompanied by the terrible abuse and jokes that ordinary people are capable of. Some of their *hajv* poems are slanderous, often indecent, full of offence, and generally characterised by hetero- and homosexual obscenities, offending honour and morality. Despite this, even serious and respectable people may be attracted to that world and secretly delight in and enjoy those pleasantries.[67]

Authors and Texts

To present our corpus in a balanced and unbiased way, we felt that the authors should speak for themselves. We thus decided to translate a series of texts representing the *hajv/hazl* phenomenon as a whole. This selection takes into account the various factors to be highlighted (authors, periods, themes, poetic forms and significance). We present 169 compositions by 65 poets making a total of 1,628 lines.[68] Classifying them chronologically we have the following groups:[69]

10th century: ʿAbbâsi, Abu ʿÂsem, ʿAmmâre, Kesâʾi, Maʿrufi, Monjik, Morâdi, Rudaki, Shahid and Tayyân (10 poets and 20 compositions totalling 23 lines);

11th century: ʻAsjadi, Dibâji, Gorgâni, Kâferak, Labibi, Lâmeʻi, Manuchehri, Masʻud-e Saʻd, Nâser-e Khosrow and ʻOmar Khayyâm (10 poets and 30 compositions totalling 169 lines);
12th century: Abu ʼl-ʻAlâʼ, Adib Sâber, ʻAmʻaq, Anvari, Asir od-Din-e Akhsikati, ʻAttâr, Ebn-e Khatib, Jamâl od-Din, Khâqâni, Mahsati, Mojir od-Din, Mokhtâri, Nezâmi-ye ʻAruzi, Nezâmi-ye Ganjavi, Qamar, Rashidi, Ruhi, Sanâʼi, Shamsi ʼl-Aʻraj, Sharaf od-Din Yahyâ al-ʻOwfi, Shatranji, Suzani, Vatvât and Zahir od-Din-e Fâryâbi (24 poets and 73 compositions totalling 683 lines);
13th century: Badr-e Jâjarmi, Farghâni, Homâm, Kamâl od-Din, Nezâri, Pur-e Bahâ, Qomri, Rumi and Saʻdi (9 poets and 22 compositions totalling 443 lines);
14th century: ʻÂref-e Ardabili, Ebn-e Yamin, Hâfez, Khâju, ʻObeyd, Owhadi and Salmân (7 poets and 18 compositions totalling 221 lines);
15th century: Âgahi, Bâbâ Sowdâʼi, Boshâq, Jâmi and Qâri (5 poets and 6 compositions totalling 89 lines).

Regarding the poetic forms, they are mainly *qetʻe* but there are also several examples of *masnavi* and *qaside*, various *robâʻi*, some ghazals, a *tarjiʻband* and many single lines.

The selection was made by scrutinising divans, dictionaries, *tazkere*[70] and anthologies, initially ignoring typological classifications.[71] At a subsequent stage, the selected corpus was divided, bearing in mind the genres listed at the beginning of the introduction. We have thus established three main categories of poems.

Two categories include compositions reflecting a critical and censorious approach to people or human contexts.

The first of these two categories consists of poems in which the author's attitude varies from hostility towards behaviour or actions that he condemns as offensive, depraved, evil or unpleasant, to amusement at something he considers ridiculous and absurd, with all the shades of meaning in between. These compositions all contain, albeit with various degrees of intensity, elements not only of aggression or derision but also of judgement and denunciation. They have been defined in our classification as 'satirical poetry' and include, at one extreme, serious social criticism, and at the other a playful, jocular treatment along the lines of comedy. This is the largest category and amounts to 109 compositions totalling 1,261 lines.

The second category is made up of compositions which, while still showing a critical and aggressive attitude, clearly lack an element of judgement and denunciation. They have been defined as 'invective poetry'. This category also includes compositions technically described as imprecatory, ranging from simple ill-wishing to vitriolic cursing. In this category there are 49 compositions and 126 lines.

The third and last category includes compositions in which the critical comments are directed at literary phenomena instead of human subjects. They are witty, amusing compositions about forms, styles, genres and poetic procedures in the serious tradition and have been defined as 'burlesque poetry'. This category has 11 compositions and 241 lines.

We must point out that various compositions, although clearly ascribable to one of the three categories, may also contain elements that are typical of the other two, and so with, for example, invective and imprecatory poetry characterized by traits of satire and burlesque. This confirms what we said initially about the difficulty of making clear-cut distinctions between such typological labels. Nonetheless, the three categories of satirical, invective/imprecatory and burlesque poetry do make a useful reference point for an overall interpretation of the structure of the corpus.

Following this logic, and wishing to frame in more detail the mechanisms of our selected poems, we have also made subdivisions in each of the three categories according to the textual and extra-textual features described in the introduction. Satirical poems have thus been grouped in relation to the *mahju*;[72] invective and imprecatory poetry by theme; and burlesque poetry according to the literary phenomenon involved.

As for the subject matter, invective and imprecatory poetry turns out to be the simplest and most linear, while satirical and burlesque poetry are increasingly elaborate and complex. This led us to deal first with invective and imprecatory poetry, then satirical and lastly burlesque.[73]

Although chronologically limited to the period from the 10th to the 15th centuries, the corpus presented here turns out to be significant in terms of both quantity and quality. The tradition continued into the following centuries (see, for example, the important texts in the Qajar and Constitutional periods) and right up to the present day. Very popular among authors in every age, and an integral and vital part of Persian literary history, this poetry of censure and criticism, especially its main aspects dealt with here, namely, invective, satire and burlesque, can take its rightful place alongside the other more celebrated and more closely studied genres, such as lyric, panegyric, epic and mystical poetry. In addition to historical and linguistic factors, many of these poems also deserve to be read for their technical and aesthetic achievement, which sets them among the masterpieces of Persian literature.[74]

CHAPTER 1

Invective Poetry

Physical Images

Invective poetry is often organised round static physical images of the *mahju*. Although very much the minority, some images are actually realistic in approach:

> A stench comes from your mouth,
> you're old and have lost your hair.[75] *Tayyân*

In general, however, we find caricatured descriptions that tend to mock faults or defects:

> You are a paralytic frog, a wilted lettuce leaf,
> yet you would like to soar up like a swallow.[76] *Labibi*

Such chastened restraint in this kind of composition is the exception rather than the rule. Realistic pictures and caricatures are often characterised by outrageous and obscene elements, such as scandalous descriptions of a scatological or sexual nature, thus amplifying the offensive effect:

> You have a dried-up arse, you are decrepit and gangling,
> you are like a ripped-up sack completely covered in shit.[77] *Monjik*

> Hey you, that yellow face on your scraggy neck
> is a lank thing stuck onto another lank thing.
>
> When your mother held you in her belly,
> she kept crashing to the ground from pain:
>
> nine months of terrible pain on your account, but it was all in vain,
> since she didn't push you out of her cunt but spat you from her arse.[78]
> *Sanâ'i*

The tendency to outrageous caricature is what distinguishes most of the physical descriptions in the invective texts. The focus is on the sexually significant parts of the male body, frequently at the centre of comic comparisons:

How can I describe your arse? Come on tell me, O you
who are better than Bayâni and Bu 'l-Horr at writing poetry![79]

And although it is difficult even for someone like you,
you might think of a bloated camel yawning in Spring.[80] *Labibi*

Your balls have become like a mortar,
they are coloured like a pan's underbelly.[81] *Tayyân*

The role of the genitalia dominates this kind of poetry to such an extent that grotesque descriptions of them, in the second half of the comparison, may irreverently cast light on serious and even symbolic elements associated with the *mahju*, as in the following line:

That red turban he wears on his head
is like a nasty wart on the tip of a cock.[82] *Morâdi*

A minor role is given to other parts of the body, usually described in more restrained language, as in the next two poems, in which we find direct references to the degradation of hygienic standards (we will describe them in more detail below):

You're like a dirty toad and, just like a toad,
your eyes bulge as if you were being strangled.

How much longer will you continue to hang round me?
You are filthier and more contemptible than a toad![83] *Labibi*

Look at the thousand signs of impurity that are on Mo'in,
the poor wretch is so unlucky, with his pox-blistered face.

His ugly face is also filthy: it's like a skimmer
in Nimrod's kitchen, but used only for ashes.[84] *Âgahi*

The beard is of special interest. In general, its symbolic value is degraded through various forms of caricature. There are few descriptions that could be defined as respectable:

His beard is much longer by far than his stature,
a hundred grim spiders have made their webs in it.[85] *Maʿrufi*

The beard is often linked with obscene elements and contexts. It may, for example, be associated with the hairs on the male pubes:

Your face can't be seen under that puny beard,
just as a pansy's cock is lost in his pubic hair.[86] *Monjik*

The beard is also mentioned with the female organ, and the situation is even more outrageous if the organ in question belongs to an animal, as in these lines in which the degradation of the grotesquely described beard is part of a larger joke:

The beard round the mouth of our malevolent guide
is a web that has been woven on the cunt of a cow.

His bald head with those few straggly hairs
looks like a dried-out gourd with fly shit on it.

At birth, they severed his head instead of his umbilical cord,
now they should cut that cord by bursting up through his arse.[87]
Anvari

The posterior, with its unpleasant hairiness and embarrassing flatus, may also be worked into a startling play with the beard:

A single hair taken from a poor wretch's arse
is more precious than a ton of hairs in his beard:

if a horse blanket were woven from that beard,
a yard of its cloth would not be worth a single fart.[88] *Khâju*

The image of the beard is also used as the main reference in violating the taboo of uncleanliness, both as regards excrement and by combining excrement with other bodily fluids:

That beard is like a brush well hardened with starch,
you would think shit had been rubbed on it all night.[89] *'Ammâre*

That face and beard soaked in shit, phlegm and slaver
remind me of dung beetles squashed under one's feet.[90] *Labibi*

Excrement and bodily fluids are often part of the violation of hygienic mores. Together with the caricaturing of the human body (with which it is often inextricably linked), this violation is another topos characterising physical descriptions in invective poetry. There are many specific references to bodily fluids, such as eye rheum:

That filthy eye is so heavily clogged with rheum,
you would think two owls have nested there.[91] *'Ammâre*

or nasal mucus:

Your nose is exactly like a Kurdish house,
always stuffed with curd and sour milk.[92] *'Ammâre*

There are also descriptions combining more than one of these fluids:

He has two streams of snot constantly running down
into his mouth, and two crops of rheum in his eyes.[93] *Shahid*

Anyone seeing you will immediately begin to retch
at the snot and slaver dribbling on your face and chest.[94] *Shahid*

But in terms of anti-hygiene, excrement and the related context play a leading role:

Those who called you 'turf face' were quite right,
that name is no exaggeration for a bastard like you.

You should know, however, that, of all the turf in the world,
your face reminds us of that where an arse has been wiped.[95] *Monjik*

Obviously the stench of excrement is also mentioned, being the archetypal example of the worst of smells, as in these lines in which sexual insult and the scatological aspect are strictly linked:

The stench coming from your mouth is so powerful,
in that gruesome body, that when my cock fucks you,

making a huge shit drop out, one never knows
whether it'll be from your arse or your mouth.[96] *Qomri*

In addition to these typical miasmas, there are other equally noxious effluvia associated with the sexually significant parts of the body:

Your mouth infects the wine and the cup,
you stink like a cesspool from head to foot.

You may well have an arse of high-quality camphor,
but your cock is like an ape's rank-smelling carcass.[97] *Qomri*

Some mention is also made of odours coming from other zones of the body:

Not even if you decided to sew a musk pouch[98]
to your armpit would that stench in there diminish.[99] *'Ammâre*

Actions Involving the Victims of Satire

In various cases, rather than emphasising static physical imagery, the poet describes actions undertaken by the *mahju*, or actions to his detriment. These more narrative contexts encourage, within the context of invective poetry, features we described as satirical, confirming the inextricable links between our genres. Deeds attributed to the *mahju* are repeatedly associated with uncleanliness:

He's a filthy wretch, dirtying the whole city,
a cow fouling other cows with her dung.[100] *Rudaki*

That dog and bigot gives me the services
I usually receive from my snots and slavers.[101] *'Asjadi*

The *mahju*'s actions also reveal his sexual depravity. There are many references to 'passive' attitudes:

My lord hankers after cocks so much
that his table is only laid with sausages.[102] *Maʿrufi*

True lords bestow their goods on pilgrims and beggars,
your money goes to the cobbler to make you a leather cock.[103]
Abu ʿÂsem

There is also no lack of 'active' vices:

Rabid, he sank his teeth into his sister's cunt,
like a dervish pulling up his threadbare cloak.[104] *Labibi*

O my king, if you wish to know absolutely everything
about this Bu ʾl-Hakam, remember he fucks jackasses.

And when he's at home, and finds nothing else,
I'm convinced he also fucks walls and doors.

Don't call that impudent oaf by the name of son,
he even fucks his wretched ninety-year-old father.[105]
Asir od-Din-e Akhsikati

In most cases the addressees are males, but at times reference to females is also explicit:

O you who shaved each last hair grown on your cunt,[106]
and, wearing your veil, gave it away with fake moans,

throw your cunt to the dogs! This poet's cock
is really horrified by depraved women's cunts.[107] *Kesâʾi*

There are also examples of sexual aberrations of both males and females being mentioned together. In the following example, the affront is extended to a whole family:

For a very long time during his youth, that pansy Najib
blithely gave his arse as his six sons have done after him.

Now that he is an old man in a different state,
he has opened a shop selling household cunts.[108] *Shatranji*

Even marital love provides interesting material for degrading and offensive interpretations:

> That son shat out by Mo'jezi's wife
> is a miracle worked by Mo'jezi himself:
>
> spineless, dirty and lecherous,
> really a dull, stuttering beanpole.
>
> Mo'jezi has a genius for everything,
> thanks to his quite extraordinary skills.
>
> Otherwise whoever would know how
> to stick a donkey's cock up a cow's cunt?[109] *Sanâ'i*

Even in those cases when the actions attributed to the *mahju* do not violate taboos concerning hygiene or sex, his honour is still sullied:

> When he raises his voice, he's like a bawling camel,
> he eats only roots and leeks, and does nothing but burp.[110] *Labibi*

At times poets find ways of sullying the honour of the *mahju* even when he has positive traits, which are mentioned in these contexts not so much to give rise to effective praise as to create a humorous and ironical sketch:

> You are crabbed and sourly but that phrase of yours is wonderful,
> you have certainly given us a phrase that is worthy of great praise.
>
> A precious saying came out of your mouth:
> a pearl dropped from a donkey's arsehole.[111] *Homâm*

Actions perpetrated to the detriment of the *mahju* may be classified in a similar way. At times they violate hygienic norms, as in these lines which also deal with the topos of insults concerning the beard:

> O Kamâl-e Sab'i, if I made *hajv* on you,
> I would end up injuring my own tongue.
>
> If I said you were as ugly as a bear,
> I would give offence to the poor bear.

And if I expressed the wish that your beard rest
on my arse, it would be a terrible fate for my arse.

All that I can do is shit on your beard,
but only after taking a strong purgative.[112] *Anvari*

On other occasions the insults and aggression are aimed at the sexual sphere of the victim:

That unhappy donkey should not be reproached,
if the further I put it up him the more he kicks out:

I know very well what part of his body is ticklish,
when I touch him down there, he bursts out laughing.[113] *Labibi*

At times the themes of violation of hygienic norms and sexual depravity occur together, with the beard and pubes always playing leading roles:

When I went to Guzgânân I found there[114]
a bearded prince and a catamite minister.

I also saw two things that were wasted atop of another two things:
a fart on the beard of the first and a cock in the arse of the second.[115]
Sanâ'i

Imprecatory Poetry

As far as imprecatory poetry is concerned, the ill-wishing and cursing are also associated with violations of the taboos concerning hygiene and sex:

May I always see you hanging with your head down like a cock,
may I always see you with your mouth full of shit like an arse,

may I always see you outside every entrance like a pair of balls,
may I always see you drowning in blood like a menstruating cunt.[116]
'Obeyd

Maledictions concerning relatives of the victim are particularly common and usually have sexual implications:

O lord, how cold and cruel you are! May what has the length
and thickness of a massive rope be stuck up your son's arse![117] *'Abbâsi*[118]

I won't make *hejâ* on your mother,
because your mother is too virtuous:

a cock up to the balls and a foot up to the knee
deep inside the cunt of your brother's mother![119] *Adib Sâber*

This use of paraphrasing to insult and curse the mother of the *mahju* is no isolated example. Here is another case, preceded by a malediction against the *mahju*, again concerning the uncleanliness of his beard:

Hey Se Busesh, I will make *hejâ* on you,
and it will be nice, I swear it on your head:

may your beard be in the cunt of a menstruating woman,
and a donkey's cock in the cunt of your father's wife![120] *Sanâ'i*

The beard is also the key element in a more moderate kind of malediction, in which the unusual *mahju* is the beloved:

Take a look at his beauty and his charms,
his deceits, his tricks, his bullying of lovers,

and then his arrogant bragging: 'I do not have any beard!'
O Lord, strike him on the neck with that sword: the beard![121] *Mahsati*

Composite Poetry

Mainly because of its brevity, the invective and imprecatory poetry presented so far usually contains and illustrates straightforward subjects and is generally focused on a single theme. In longer poems, the motifs (physical images, actions, etc.) are more numerous and may also appear intertwined and mixed, giving rise to a composite picture. We find various levels of thematic complexity, with a potential, consequent increase in the satirical features.

At times there are only a few well-defined subjects, as in this *qet'e* in which the figurative description of the sexual abuses perpetrated on the *mahju* is accompanied by a final curse on him:

O you catamite Kamâl, to let my cock up into you,
your arse has become as wide as my palace courtyard.

The dance at our sovereign's feast grew more lively,
the more my flute blew and puffed up your bagpipe.

Frequently the cock that sits between my legs
slipped into that eye you have in your rear.

And how often I tied my balls to your neck,
like bells that are hung to embellish a camel!

You told me not to dishonour you with my *hejâ*:
may my *hejâ* moisten the arse of your honour![122] *Qomri*

The following three compositions are based on a model similar to the previous poem, with a few variations. In the first example there is again a description of sexual abuses perpetrated on the *mahju*, but this time the final curse is extended to the wife:

O ʿÂrefak, they stuck a wick in your arse: that's why your title is 'Lantern'![123]
And every night, until my death, I will pour all my yogurt into you like oil.

Here I deal with cocks: keep your wife away from me,
so that you won't be covered by the dirt of offence!

I had promised not to say it, but now I will: a donkey's cock!
How far up? To the balls! Where? In your wife's arse and cunt![124]
Shamsi ʾl-Aʿraj

In the next case, the ill-wishing is at the beginning and this time is not sexual in nature, while the perversion concerns the *mahju*'s wife:

Sit down and listen to these three lines of *hajv* from me,
you'll be so angry your eyes will bulge from their sockets.

What you have often seen first-hand in your own wife,
has never been told in the world, not even of Shalfiyye.[125]

It would seem she has no rivals,
in truth, that's the way it really is:

in being a great cuckold and husband of a whore,
you will only see your equal if you look in a mirror.[126]

Nezâmi-ye 'Aruzi

In the third example the illicit sexual practices of both the *mahju* and his wife are described with a final curse on both:

Your wife, O Falak, is a great cock-eater,
she's a whore and bastard just like you!

A mule has never given birth: how come
your wife lusts so much after a donkey's cock?

Your arse is wrecked and you're a living offence to all donkeys,[127]
how can it be that your wife's cunt and arse are so wrecked?

I have unstitched the buttonhole of her cunt so much,
that you'll never be able to sew it up with your needle.

I am not Suzani but, with my poems,[128]
I can make cocks rain on your hole.

Just like you, may your wife be down
on all fours like a dog at every crossroad![129] *Qamar*

The thematic structure can also be more complicated than the cases presented so far. In the next poem, for instance, the details of the *mahju*'s depravity, with the usual final curse, are heightened by a physical and moral caricature:

You really are a midget, you're so minute
that people think you're a weird chubby doll.

You get smaller by the second: how strange,
perhaps God makes you sink into the earth?

If they shaved off your beard and moustache,
you would easily be taken for a little baby.

You only offer bread to someone who gives you
his cock: you enjoy his cock and he your bread.

Let the teeth be sharp by day and the cock strong by night,
of him who eats all your bread and then bursts your arse.

You are such a cold scoundrel that if you shed a single tear
in the Tigris, the river would freeze even in mid-Summer.[130] *Lâmeʿi*

The next two compositions are even more elaborate. In the first, not only are the taboos of uncleanliness and nudity violated but degrading physical defects, slanderous moral features and the *mahju*'s sexual perversions are also highlighted:

You stink much worse than ten-day-old stew in Summer,
and you're blinder than a corpse after a year in the tomb.

That bun on your tablecloth resembles a child's shit,
the soup in your bowl looks like a drunk's vomit.

Only when it's not time to eat you promise your food,
your table has no bread, just like the beggar's board.

Your arse is like a bitch's cunt: when a cock gets up it,
a thousand tricks and efforts are required to pull it out.

Nonetheless, night and day you lust for a cock,
just like a suckling baby is always craving the tit.[131] *Lâmeʿi*

In the following composition, thanks to its greater length, the list of themes is further extended. We find offensive descriptions of physical features (both realistic and caricatured), moral condemnation, sexual outrage, violations of the taboo of uncleanliness, insults to relatives, curses and a finale which, alluding to the corresponding models in serious poetry, gives a certain burlesque feel to the whole poem:

Hey Oghol, you have a stinking beard and fetid armpits,
that mouth of yours chews dog shit all through the night.

Everybody else usually shits from their arse, but you
shit from your mouth, your arse and your armpits.

Before the sovereign, you are like the devil with Adam,
at banquets you are like a pagan idol in the Kaaba.

Thinking of you is thinking of death,
you are a paragon of the worst luck.

You are corpulent, disgusting and foul like poverty and penury,
lowly-bred and evil-natured, you're as despicable as mock gold.

In Ghur a crowd of people like you are worth a few handfuls of flour,
and in India a herd of people like you can be bought for half a seed.[132]

For sure you are a great man! The dowry of your mother
was a thousand one-eyed cats and blotchy-legged dogs.

If you lined up the swarms of lice under your trouser belt,
all the motes in the world would not rival their ranks.

I pray you get paralysed, you bald trollop and husband of a whore!
Because of you, my joy's head is bald and my pleasure's hand is numbed.

Your mouth resembles a head, your head a beard and your beard an arse,
your heart is like hell and those two cheeks of yours are like hairy velvet.

It could be said that God, be He honoured and glorified,
created you from precious essences and delicate elements:

from the earth of suffering, the water of poverty, the fire of pain,
from a great shit, the roots of cock hairs, the stench of armpits.

Every night you drag your wife under the Antichrist's donkey,[133]
so that he floods her with his sperm and drowns her in mud.

Hey two-legged dog, you are like the sun, which moves
from East to West, at times in Pisces, at times in Aries.

Not every baldy is a pansy like you,
many pansies at least are not bald.

Your wife is just like your mother: two great whores!
Your father is just like you: both with stinking armpits!

The hooks of a saddlebag, a donkey's cock and a camel's leg
would be lost in a corner of the crack in your mother's cunt.

Your are like a drawing that death shaped on the features of misfortune
and was traced in shit by the devil on the face of ill-omened Saturn.

That beard of yours makes you look like a drowned bear,
the tip of your moustache looks like a bent thorn on a hilltop.

Your lips and teeth are really wretched:
pottery shards stuck into a dung-heap.

You are a bastard with a hunch on your back, you're grim like misbelief,
you have the strength of an ant, and resemble a snake or ill-omened Saturn.

You receive your daily bread by your arse and your wife's cunt,
I get gifts from the king for my poetry, be it serious, witty or amatory.

You're the colour of rotten roots and stink like an onion,
you're like bile in the body and like a spike in the eye.

Know that man reaches maturity thanks to distance:
journeying raises man from wretchedness to nobility.

People living far from home are even more worthy than martyrs,
thus spoke the Light of the Holy Law, our prophet Muhammad.

Journeying brings grace, happiness and honour,
journeying brings perfection, greatness and dignity.

If I had never felt the distance and separation from the homeland,
when would I have had the honour of serving the Pillar of Fortune?[134]

'Am'aq

CHAPTER 2

Satirical Poetry

Patrons and Ruling Classes

In this kind of compositions, the most common attitude towards patrons (sovereigns, princes, ministers, etc., whose names may or may not be mentioned) is that of disappointment and criticism for not having granted the poet the gifts that he expected. The gifts have often been requested by the poet himself and sometimes promised by the patron, as in the following example:

In my life I have composed and recited numerous poems,
one after the other, with care, for my lord Seqat ol-Molk.

Like a branch that is weighed down heavily with many hopes,
I entered his service, but that branch dried up and bore no fruit.

He made claims to being a poet, but didn't know the art,
and despite this, out of sheer ignorance, he even bragged.

I have never seen nor heard of a greater cow than him,
fate was mistaken in granting him such fine fortune.

Alas, that I ever placed my hopes in that great cuckold!
Alas, that I ever wasted my poems on that son of a whore![135] *Gorgâni*

The last lines reveal how the poet may even be so audacious as to insult his patron. Notwithstanding the obvious risks, his reaction is characterised by outrageous abuse. Here are another two examples. In the first, the offence is directed at the patron's wife:

Considering character and nature,
your wife's arse is worthier than you:

you never meet my requests,
but it always satisfies my cock.[136] *Sanâ'i*

In the second example, the poet insults and humiliates the patron himself, emphasising his insolence through ironic self-imprecation:

I wrote this panegyric for an unworthy man
from whom I received no reward of any kind:

a fart straight in my beard as the panegyrist,
a cock in the arse of him whom I praised![137] *Anvari*

In addition to insults, the disappointed poet may even make threats. The patron's wife is also often at the centre of such menacing:

You bent your back like a tent
under a thousand muleteers.

You have driven to starvation
many artists with deceit and lies.

Your face is as sour as yogurt soup,
for how much longer will you frown?

You are a cuckold, who sells his wife and even cheats,
and, if you reply, I'll fuck your wife just as the others do![138]
Zahir od-Din-e Fâryâbi

But the threats are more frequently directed at the patron and involve writing *hajv*:

O lord, in waiting for your gifts,
I have definitely lost my patience.

Panegyrists usually write three pieces of poetry:
the first is panegyric, the second expresses a request,

and, if met, a laud ensues as the third, otherwise you get lines of *hejâ*.
I have already written the first two; what would you like for the third?[139]
Kamâl od-Din

In some cases the threats to the patron are mixed with the usual offences:

O Hamid od-Din, you are a great sun of generosity,
let not death come to your banquet before its time!

You promised me some cane sugar, which I never got.
Remember I am a poet, and I write both *madh* and *hejâ*.

For now I will merely remind you of the donkey's cock,
but, if I don't get my dues, I'll say where that cock is![140] *Anvari*

Faced with the patron's indifference, and to obviate the consequent economic difficulties, *hajv* is often seen as the only possible solution:

O my lord, for over a year I have been drinking
the wine of your praise from the cup of poetry.

But I have not seen even a morsel of bread,
nor have I received a rag with which to dress.

If I were asked in a gathering about your generosity,
I would certainly have to put cotton in my ears.

I am reflective, good and silent
because of my generous nature,

but, when I begin to write poetry,
people always proudly put me first:

because of my *madh* and *hajv*, for thanks and complaints,
I shine brightly like the sun or thunder like the ocean.

If you give me no reward for my *madh* to you,
I will not grow sad or angry on that account.

I only need to read a line or two of *hajv* about you,
and I am immediately presented with a brocade.

In exchange for such *hejâ*, I can get pure gold,
it's thus quite obvious why I sell it so dearly.[141] *Zahir od-Din-e Fâryâbi*

When, as a sign of extreme disdain, the poet declares he no longer wants to waste *madh* or even *hajv* on his patron, he does so in a kind of particularly caustic *hajv*:

He'd like all the poets in the world to be always
at his table, singing his praises with no reward.

By God, he must truly be great, wise and noble,
if everyone has to write him panegyrics for free!

But I won't write *madh* to him as it would sully my mind,
and I won't wear out my tongue reciting *hajv* about him.

Madh of that wrecked-arsed donkey would be false,
and *hajv* on that great cuckold would be a real waste.[142] *Sanâ'i*

The threat can also develop into an invitation to abandon miserly, petty patrons who, in the following passage, are contrasted with generous kings:

Every master of the art of eloquence
found honour with the munificent king.

You, too, always hover round him!
There you'll find gold and money!

Why bring bunches of flowers
to the seed-seller in the alley?

Don't ask for clothes from those who are so greedy
as to steal the patches from their fathers' breeches.

Why do you compose poems for doormen and guards?
Do you want to be left in the corridor, like a pair of shoes?

When you kiss a lip, you will find sweet sugar,
if you kiss an arse, what will you find? A fart![143] *Sanâ'i*

Rarer, and less significant in this context, are some moderately constructive complaints:

If my lord overlooks and forgets me,
I send him a note to refresh his memory.

If the suckling babe doesn't start crying,
he'll get no loving milk from his mother.[144] *Shahid*

The main cause of the patron's reluctance to satisfy the poets, provoking their discontent, is usually attributed to his stinginess, which is described in more or less irreverent tones:

> Our lord owns goods and riches,
> no one ever enjoys that fortune.
>
> But he is always so tight-fisted that he will not even allow
> the bath-attendant to touch his dirt or the barber his hair.[145] *ʿAsjadi*

> Stinginess makes our lord colder
> than snow in the freezing Winter:
>
> he's so mean he won't stick all
> of his cock up his wife's cunt.[146] *Kâferak*

A lord may also give the poet a gift, but if it is of poor quality, again a series of complaints will ensue:

> O Sire, you promised me a horse,
> and the word of my king is sacred.
>
> But they gave me a really old black nag and I thought
> there couldn't be a black horse as old as it in the world.
>
> I gave it back to receive another,
> hoping that no one would notice.
>
> But I didn't get a horse of a different hue:
> beyond black there is no other colour![147] *Salmân*

> I sang you many lines of praise,
> gems paraded at every gathering.
>
> In exchange you gave me a robe of honour like genitals:
> I have to keep it well concealed in front of everybody.[148] *Kamâl od-Din*

Among the more frequent and more elaborate protests of these kinds are those concerning wine given as a gift by the patron, as in the next two poems, the second characterised by a curious sequence of curses:

I had asked for some wine from Razi od-Din,
he promised to give me it, but much time passed.

Yesterday evening he suddenly decided to keep his vow,
I was full of joy, and the night was shaping up as a feast day.

But then a young servant came forward with a small bottle,
so small that it certainly could be of no use whatsoever.

Inside was stinking, nauseating juice with a nasty colour,
almost as if they had poured a draught of pus into the cup.

It was like dregs mixed with sawdust,
crumbs of dung dissolved in horse piss.

Right off I said to the servant: 'Take it back, and tell our lord
I really did not expect such great courtesy from his generosity!

They must have procured this wine from the worst of possible places!'
He replied: 'Of course! It comes from the barrel of our glorious lord!'[149]

Kamâl od-Din

From the one and only Sa'd od-Din As'ad,
two jars of wine we asked for the three of us,

to drink, with four other companions,
five cups of clear wine all at once.

But he sent us some six-year-old wine,
and all our seven members were dazed.[150]

And so our gathering, which was like the eight paradises,
became a source of suffering like the nine celestial vaults.[151]

May ten men take him off to the tomb,
and his moustache go up eleven arses,

may twelve members of his family be ruined,
and thirteen of his female relatives be sullied,

may fourteen farts let rip and strike his beard,
and fifteen hairs be torn from his moustache![152]

Mojir od-Din

As in invective poetry, in this context we also come across compositions with a more complex thematic structure. In the next poem, the author complains in great detail about his state of neglect and then abuses and curses a patron before moving on—through a classical-style passage—to praise another patron in the final lines:

In this world I have neither gold nor silver,
my balls are squashed and my cock is bare.

I'm a shield rained on by affliction's stones,
and a censer for the fire of great suffering.

I offer my flank to the kicks of poverty,
and my chin to the punches of injustice.

Like a cock, I am worthy of a place of honour,
but like balls I have to stay outside every door.

I can't hang about with dignitaries,
because poetry is my bow and quiver.

I would behave like Abu Nuwâs: when I fuck,[153]
I hold boys' buttocks in the palm of my hand,

and when it comes to boisterous feasts,
my thighs make cushions for their arses.

Thanks to my cock, like sewing thread,
I could be a needle pushing into clothes.

My cock is held tight and suffocates,
even when I fuck the most wrecked cunts.

But since, like a man mirrored in water,
my big cock's destiny is upside down,

I only manage to fuck a beautiful boy
by taking advantage when he's asleep.

I don't have enough money to wash myself,
my clothes are worn out, like a piece of soap:

they are completely tattered and torn,
and look like sores after blood-letting.

That is what my clothes are like, and my food
is no better: raw lung is like roast chicken for me.

The town of Nishapur is a very inhospitable place,
and I survive thanks to aromas of distant tables.

Instead of soft bread, all I have is hard leather.
Not surprising, since I'm the guest of a cobbler.

I am like a prisoner kept in the palace
of that pansy prince, Mohammad Âshu.

He is always muttering away in a low voice:
'I'm one of the most powerful men in all Iran.'

Thanks to my poetic talent, before him
I am like Rostam in the hour of battle.[154]

I have fucked every one of his great heroes,
I'm like Sâm the head-slicer, Narimân's son.[155]

If he wishes to wage war on me,
I have no need of deceit and ruses:

to avoid the blows of his red-hot sword,
I'm well-protected by a helmet and armour.

One evening he said to me: 'Hey, get up,
and soothe the itch I have here behind!'

I gave him this for an answer: 'That ring
on your secret door has blunted my sharp file.'[156]

Then he said: 'With the fine-tuned needle of your scales,
I implore you, weigh the goods that I have in my back-shop!'

I answered him: 'My scales, O great lord,
can't take the weight of stones and pebbles.'

And since I didn't stick my club into his bag,
he didn't give me any fresh bread for my bag.

I can't see either table or cups anywhere around him,
my hand reaches nothing, it's as short as the foot of a tray.

If I'm not telling the truth, may his wrecked arse
be stuck right up to the hilt of my hairy cock!

But I no longer want to talk of that wretch.
I even regret everything I have ever said.

Instead, I implore you with heart and soul,
since in time of pain you are my only salve.

As long as one can pray to his lord,
I will frequent no other court than yours.

May your door be open to fortune,
and my heart and soul bound to you.

In the garden of service to you, my pact
and pledge are as fresh as the rose and tulip.[157] *Ruhi*

There are also rarer cases in which the poet's resentment towards his patron is not clearly stated and the satirical aspect is played down in favour of pure invective:

Whenever I enter my lord's chamber,
that pansy never gets up in front of me.

He's frightened that a lot of cocks will fall from his arse,
and there will be no place anywhere near him left for me.[158] *Kâferak*

Occasionally, the satire of the powerful is not directly connected to personal disappointment, but rather takes on the more general tones of an underlying basic discontent:

One day a prince met his death in Isfahan,
one of those princes who had risen to power.

I saw his coffin carried on the shoulders of the bath attendants,
and was amazed: I couldn't understand what they were doing.

I asked a man: 'Why have the bath attendants
now started carrying coffins down here?

In every city gravediggers are a separate guild,
and every one must stick to his own trade.'

He pulled on his moustache and said: 'As far as I know,
the bath attendants have always carried the rubbish away.'[159] *Khâju*

The whole ruling class may be the subject of similar discontent:

> The city of Bâvard is in every way like a watermill:[160]
> the wheel is all pain and the canal made of suffering.
>
> Its prefect is a dog, the judge is an ass,
> the governor a camel and the taxman a cow.
>
> And what's the fate of its people?
> Only beatings, taxes and insults![161] *Bâbâ Sowdâ'i*

In line with the spirit of these two last compositions, in which there are no more private and self-interested aspects, we find serious and committed protests addressed to the suffering wrought on subjects by tyrants. They are much nearer to a social critique than to pure satire. Some of these protests are permeated with a resigned pessimism:

> Will wheat ever cost as much again as a bar of cheap soap,
> given that its price now belittles that of pearls from Oman?
>
> My heart has shrunk to a seed for lack of bread,
> thinking of wheat has turned me into a poor wretch.
>
> Once there was bread and faith in people's mouths,
> now, not even at the price of faith can you obtain wheat.
>
> A small locust came from Khorasan and immediately
> gobbled up all the wheat in the realm of Qohestân.
>
> But the tyrants, made shrewder by the harsh times,
> have heaped up big piles of wheat in the granaries,
>
> and have no intention of giving it to the hungry,
> unless in exchange for gold, jewels and silver.
>
> They wouldn't grant a single seed to the needy,
> not even if wheat rained from the sky like water.
>
> This is a time of ill-starred destiny and of calamity,
> and if you find wheat at the price of your life, it's cheap.
>
> Before this great catastrophe came, we were never aware
> that wheat could be as dear as the heartbreaker and the soul.

However, Nezâri would never request from those cowards
a gift of wheat, even if he were about to die a hundred times.[162] *Nezâri*

In other poems the accusations levelled at tyrants and their condemnation is accompanied by a spirit of rebellion and faith in better times:

O my friend, I'm utterly dejected,
and my innermost heart aches.

The pain for so many bewildered people
has taken hold in my anguished soul.

The kingdom in the hands of these oppressors
is as if it were tied under an elephant's foot.

They have renounced the real faith,
and, like pagans, attack all Muslims.

Look! They are scorpions in people's food,
they are worms boring their way into meat.

Or, rather, you'd say that these oppressors are dogs,
snatching at all kinds of food in a year of famine.

They are all after wealth and power,
but are like blind men fallen into a well.

They have filled up their bellies with wine,
and, like drunks, lie on their backs in the mud.

O unhappy people, when will you eat
your fill again, if you are so starved now

by these dogs here, who are nothing more
than teeth fallen from the kingdom's mouth?

That prince, who always handed out
gold to beggars in great quantities,

now has only heaps of lice in his shirt collar,
not the fragrance of ambergris and musk.[163]

O that these plunderers and beggars
be attacked and kicked out by dogs!

They have laid people prostrate in the cold,
like snow fallen on the ground in Winter.

Alas! The authority of many princes
has passed into these beggars' hands.

The seal has slipped off Solomon's finger,
and has ended up in the hands of demons.[164]

In the arena the women now have the ball,
the stick has dropped from the hands of men.

The hunter has been trapped like a bird,
he is like a grain of wheat fed to a hen.

In the age of these dogs, the flock of sheep
is in the wolf's claws for want of a shepherd.

The citizens are the sheep, and these dogs
are wolves always pouncing on the sheep.

O Lord, send us some leopards
to attack these rabid wolves!

Because of these assassins,
the whole kingdom is in ruins.

O you, who are persecuted and smitten,
who are stunned by such suffering,

O you, who, because of the violence of such oppressors,
have been humiliated in your own city like foreigners,

have a little patience and soon you will see
these oppressors slain and their leaders routed.

Those leaders who have tormented you
will be ruined in disgrace like prisoners.

Whoever lives in this earthly house,
will fall, just as its walls will fall.

If a warrior were suddenly to appear,
you would see these leaders succumb.

And when least you expect it, the men of faith
will take their revenge on the world-worshippers.

What can they possibly know about the state,
these people who know nothing about religion?

Remember that, through God's will,
many rulers have lost their throne.

How many glorious diadems have tumbled down
from important heads to under dishonour's feet!

It only takes a sigh from you, oppressed ones, to bring down
the crown of the kingdom from the heads of these sovereigns.

Even if heaven were their throne,
and a hundred moons shone on it,

it's as if these people had already been cast down
from the heights of honour to deposition's mud.

And why do you, O Seyf -e Farghâni,
also hurt yourself in this house of pain?[165]

You are only a pawn on this chessboard, but have already seen
how many down here have fallen from the horse of fortune.

You can be sure these people will also fall,
and someone else will sit in their place.

In this garden they are like poplars without fruit,
trees that will be blown over by a breath of wind.

God will send a remedy for the people
who suffer because of this great pain.[166] *Farghâni*

Similar to these attacks are the accusations against not only the political but also the overall social establishment, at times with claims that we might in modern terms describe as existentialist:

Do you know what the harp and the lute declaim to us?
'Drink wine secretly or you will be tainted with heresy!'

They always tell us not to reveal and not to listen
to love's secret. What they recount is a difficult story!

People dishonour the dignity of love and lovers' grace,
the young are thwarted and the old are strongly rebuked.

Outside the door we were deceived in a hundred ways;
who knows what they will invent behind their veils!

They even disturb the Old Man of the Magi,[167]
look at what the disciples do to the Master!

Many honours could be bought with half a glance,
but the handsome ones hold back in this affair.

Some earnestly and eagerly seek out their friend,
whereas others simply rely upon their destiny.

Don't place your trust in today's stability,
this is a workshop where all is change!

Bring some wine, then, for if you take a closer look,
the sheikh, cleric, *mufti* and censor are all hypocrites.[168] *Hâfez*

Criticisms of authority may also ignore contemporary contexts and adopt the criteria of a moralistic and didactic outlook tending to describe the general conditions of those in power. Thus in the following lines, in which we find the topos of the madman, who, because his 'innocent' mindlessness is tolerated, can upbraid the sovereign without running risks that would otherwise be inevitable:

One day Bohlul, when he was drunk,
went to Hârun and sat on his throne.[169]

The guards beat him badly with sticks and stones,
so that he immediately started to bleed all over.

After taking all those terrible beatings,
he said: 'O Hârun, sovereign of the world,

for just one instant I sat up there on your throne,
look at the state I am in because of the blows I got!

You've been sitting there all your life,
so you'll surely be hacked to pieces!

I got my dues for no more than one instant,
poor thing, you will come off much worse!'[170] *'Attâr*

Poets

In the court setting, the poets themselves are the second category, after patrons, who are frequently the butt of satire. At times this kind of satire was encouraged by the patron. There is a significant anecdote quoted in the *Chahâr Maqâle* (12th century), whereby the sultan provoked this witty response from Rashidi about 'Am'aq, who had described his rival's poetry as lacking salt:

You criticise my poems for lack of salt,
and in this you may be perfectly right.

My poems are really like sugar and honey,
and salt certainly doesn't go well with them.

But what you write tastes of turnips and beans,
and so it's you, O cuckold, who needs the salt![171] *Rashidi*

Rivalry between poets, however, was such a deep-rooted phenomenon that it certainly did not require encouragement from the patron to occur. Poetic disputes are a feature of the whole history of Persian poetry, and we find examples both at the beginning and the end of the period considered:

If Farrokhi is now dead, why is 'Onsori not dead too?[172]
An old man lingers on and a young man has gone early.

We have lost a wise man and his departure only brings grief,
a madman is left and his permanence brings no gain at all.[173] *Labibi*

Sâghari claimed that the plagiarists took[174]
every fine idea they found in his poems.

And he was quite right in making this comment:
I have read all his poems and they have no ideas.[175] *Jâmi*

Of the satires in the early period, Manuchehri's blast against an envious poet includes a long list of the possible reasons for dispute:

Many are envious of me and I am left with no companions,
give justice to the oppressed, O glory of the Prince of believers!

The male lion is always alone and swine go in pairs,
but only God, the creator of souls, is unique and one.

My envier wishes to outdo me. He's making a mistake!
The rose that blooms before its time will soon fade.

My envier thinks he can match me in knowledge,
but someone with consumption won't grow fat.

My envier says: 'Why, when you listen to my speech,
do you bend like a bow and are ready to fly like an arrow?'

It's right to do so before such an envier: when stamped,
the reversed pattern on the seal appears the right way up.

He also says to me: 'You stole all my friends!'
But those friends were already angry with him.

Wise people stay no longer than a day with him,
nobody wants to court danger more than once.

My envier says: 'What are you doing at the king's court?'
Now the hate inspiring him is clear. Here is true ignorance!

Wherever there is a garden, there is birdsong,
and, for every bird, there is a sharp arrow.

My envier says: 'I am old and you are young,
in knowledge the young can't match the old.'

But if the wisdom of wicked people grew with age,
Satan the damned would not be more abject every day.

My envier says: 'Why are my poems
read less than yours by young people?'

My poetry is clear water, while yours is muddy.
Will people drink mud if they can have clear water?

My envier says: 'Why are you in the sovereign's service?'
Foxes are suited to the service of the lion in the forest!

The elephant herder earns a living by looking after elephants,
but we courtiers do so by obeying the king of the world.

My envier says: 'Mine is the only true poetry!' What?
People can tell the lute from the harp made by Râmtin![176]

God did not place all wisdom in only one poet,
all perfumes aren't in the musk sac from China:[177]

a poet is skilled in love lyrics, another in comparisons and panegyric,
just as a musician is good at a Qâlus tune and another at Shakkartovin.

My envier says: 'Why, at the gathering of dignitaries, do we count
for little or nothing, and you are so revered and held in high esteem?'

His words demonstrate and confirm his ignorance!
My knowledge is witness and surety for my mind.

O envious one, you will never be able to see the face of intellect,
just as the damned will never contemplate the black-eyed houris.[178]

O envious one, you are called a poet, just as I am,
but your art is feeble while mine is in good health.

Look closely! Your poetry is full of many flaws and errors,
but, on the contrary, the precious pearl must be full of grace.

It's surely better to remain in silence than to write bad lines of verse,
just as it's better not to conceive than to miscarry in the sixth month.

O envious one, since I came to the court of the sultan
you have all only protested, lamented and moaned.

If you behave like that whenever a poet is near the king,
you are bound to suffer a great deal more. Be sure!

May our king enjoy long life and be endowed with strength!
May poets always come from the ends of the earth to him!

What quarrels and arguments we had last year!
And this year you still show rancour and enmity!

Whose turn will it be next year?
With whom are you ready to fight?

In writing verse and in all the arts of poetry,
I believe you are inferior to me. This is the truth!

A year ago the king ordered you to reply to one of my poems:
you haven't done so yet. Could there be greater shame than this?

If that magnanimous sovereign had asked me to do the same,
I'd have given a powerful reply greater than all your poems!

But your poems have no value and lack sufficient weight,
so that the king, that patron of poets, orders a reply to them.

You are foolish and don't realise what everyone knows,
which is that you are not my equal in the poetic art.

I am well versed in theology, medicine and grammar,
you can't tell *dâl* from *zâl, re* from *ze* and *sin* from *shin*.[179]

I know numerous Arabic divans off by heart,
you can't even read the most famous Arabic lines.

The king of Iran invited me to Ray on an elephant,[180]
and in so many years he has not even thought of you!

I am superior to you in knowledge, you are superior to me in wealth.
But knowledge surpasses wealth, just as faith surpasses this world.

You were able to grow rich thanks to the king of kings,
otherwise you would be cleaning the gutters of Ray!

You must find some great advantages in your present condition,
or you'd go back to leading the troops of our powerful sovereign.

You show off that every year you earn
no less than three or four hundred dinars.

Despite this, you refuse to be grateful to the king of the world.
If you have had nothing good from this king, pack your bags!

Go to Shervân, where they will always give you only[181]
barley bread and pork from a pig that's been dead a month!

For my part, I wish to stay in this royal court,
I never think of Ray, Gorgân or any other place.

Who has ever seen in Ray, Gorgân or Shervân,
poets on elephants with money bags on the saddle?

All the gifts our patron offers to the weakest poets in a single day,
have never been given in a lifetime by Mo'tasem and Mosta'in.[182]

Express your sincere gratitude, then, without scrimping,
if you want good luck to grant you the king's protection.

He who is grateful is one of the noblemen,
he who is ungrateful is one of the wretched![183] *Manuchehri*

Of the great number of satires on poets composed in subsequent periods, we can quote only a few representative cases here. Amongst the most prolific authors in this field is certainly Suzani. He wrote much poetry against a poet he names as Khar-e Khomkhâne ('Tavern Donkey'),[184] like the following example, which contains the famous claim that *hajv* necessarily includes offence and insults:

What on earth is this claim you make, you old donkey,
to be a poet who routs armies and conquers countries?

If you knew the art of routing armies and conquering countries,
why would the sovereign squander his finances on soldiers?

Why would he not give you the money
to send you to war and defeat his enemies?

And if you want to rout armies and conquer countries,
why do you put off this pleasant task so much?

Leap into the saddle, but check your feet carefully,
so that you don't fall off the horse during the attack,

as you spur on your steed at great speed,
and the fistula begins to bother your arse.

Conquer, in just one assault, that land whose king
is the angel of death and whose minister is the devil.

That land is called Tavern, its cities and villages are barrels,
and you, baring your stone heart, must seal its door with pitch.

Raise your standard and, with your beard for a flap,
attack all the flies on those barrels full of wine!

When you have seized all the cities and all the villages
of that powerful country where every road leads to hell,

when you have defeated that crowded land,
then you will be given the name of army-router!

Here you are actually nothing more than a tavern poet,
whose poems are sung by tavern musicians in any old way.

That's how you emulate your father's glorious deeds,
and the devil's eye lights up at the sight of you.

You ask: 'Who is the king of poets?' And you yourself reply:
'Me, of course!' O blind-spirited, brazen fool, what pride is this?

Your being a prince among poets costs you very little:
Abu Sahl made you a prince, but of dung-carters!

There is nobody like you to be found anywhere, from Kash to Kashmir,[185]
you have garlic for teeth, your head is a turnip, your lips are eggplants.

And with my fist clenched like a turnip, I will wallop you and knock
your thirty-two teeth into your lips like garlic cloves into egg-plants.

You are a donkey-headed poet, and your desire for poetry
is just like a donkey's hankering after barley and straw.

You claim: 'Who can be my equal in drawing back the bow
of poetry? I'm as strong as Mars and have Mercury's mind!'[186]

You should know that I am able to draw the bow much better,
and defeat the archer, even if he's a champion like Zâl or Hojir.[187]

My poetry is like a delicate, full-fleshed fig,
yours is thick, dry yogurt, and the fig is better.

You are nothing but a dog and all your poems are a neck chain.
Indeed, you and your poems are worth less than a dog and a chain.

You asked me not to insult you when I am composing my *hejâ*.
What should I do? Offer you roast chicken, lamb, halva and silk?

This is certainly not advice to give to anybody,
not even to an enemy may such nasty things be said.

The wise man mixes the yeast of insult with *hajv*,
so that his spirit will be raised and grows well.

Hejâ without insults is like unleavened bread,
and unleavened bread is bad for the belly.

Anyway, the insults I aim at you are all true,
I can explain them down to every last detail.

Do you remember you gambled your arse,
and your creditors burst right through it?

You have respectable creditors, and you must give them the stake,
not only are they strong, but you agreed they should have their way.

They are all kinds of people, both distinguished and ordinary,
and because of them you always end up shouting and screaming.

They have poured so much yogurt into you from the tips of their cocks
that, when you cough, a smell of cheese comes out of your throat.

In the eyes of those who know the value of poetry,
the poet who pawns his arse is a blameworthy coward.

For many years the warriors of the faith have sung *Allâho Akbar*,
at the door of your forefathers' temple, to convert them to Islam.

Now different kinds of warriors pronounce
Allâho Akbar, and come behind you at night.

They clench their cocks like bell clappers,
and, while you sleep, play those instruments.

So you see death in a dream and, when you wake,
here is my *hajv* to interpret that terrible nightmare.

May you always worry about your daily bread and death,
may my *hajv* be your only daily bread and everyday death.

I wouldn't care if you were to live or die,
a fart in your whiskers, dead or alive![188] *Suzani*

Suzani also turned his pen against illustrious colleagues such as Sanâ'i, Mo'ezzi (d. c. 1125) and Nezâmi-ye 'Aruzi. The following is a satire, with an interesting dramatic structure, written about a poet named Nezâmi who can presumably be identified with Nezâmi-ye 'Aruzi:[189]

Even if Nezâmi is still alive, I think of him as already dead,
and dedicate to him this elegy, thus fulfilling my duty as a poet.

If I had to wait for his death to compose it,
he wouldn't hear it, and that would be a pity.

So I will declaim to him such elegant lines of verse
that he will be anxious to die so as to receive this elegy.

And I hope that, thanks to my poetry, his desire will then be satisfied,
this I yearn for at the feast with a stinking-moustached scoundrel.

He is a dog with a whore for a wife, and I hope he dies like a dog,
even though he always claims that he can challenge powerful lions.

Seeing his face gets right on my nerves,
it burdens me by day and enters my dreams.

Indeed, he appeared to me while I was sleeping,
describing his suffering and torments after his death:

'They have shut me so tight in the tomb
I don't even have enough room to fart.

I also ache all over because the angel of death
beat me with his club after questioning me.

The series of lies I told when alive
has irrevocably sent me to my fate.

They stuck the list of those lies to my pimpish neck,
and dragged me to be judged and to be punished.

I needed a long rope from the tomb to hell
to bind the bundle of the sins I had committed.

I tried to move but, since I couldn't budge,
they pushed me to burn, head down, in hell.

O what pain and punishment they inflicted
for all those lies I told to make me look good!

They put a muzzle on my mouth as people do with a dog,
but I disgust even dogs because of the garbage I have eaten.

I always bragged about my Samanid descent,[190]
but now none of them down here speaks to me.

Moreover, no one cares how much they did or possessed,
I was clearly mistaken to bind all my fortune to theirs.

And because I said that Mount Khoshk belongs to me,
the angel of death hung me up on a dried-out branch.

Then they unrelentingly threw at me
all the stones that were on that hill.

They eventually gathered a thousand faggots
from its slopes, made a pile and stuck me on top.

I was so tightly bound all round by flames up there
that I felt like a grain in the middle of a pomegranate.

I lost all hope that anyone would bring me
a little fruit and ice from the town of Mazdikat.[191]

I became like the people from Sistan,
and felt as intrepid and strong as them:

instead of ice and fruit, I feed on infernal drinks and plants,
instead of roses and herbs, I always have thorns and flames.

Here I am food for snakes and I eat only thorns,
like thorns I get broken, like snakes I live in caves.

The only relief would be to have a huge cucumber
to soothe the itching the thorns make in my arse hole,

until they put me in the saddle of that speedy horse,
the devil's cock, which is as robust as a big yoke.

Down here I've lost all my nobility and power,
and I mourn and lament about it continually.

Alas, I no longer have my gold and my villages,
my castles, my houses, my lands and my gardens!

I can't even mention the name of Mount Khoshk
without the angel stoning me, and he's quite right.

I suffer when I dream of Nishapur, its parks and its gardens,
when I think about Bukhara and about the village of Bakkâr.

My heart aches remembering the caravanserais of 'Arus and Malek,
although I obtained both of them in such a dishonourable way.

And what can I say of the falcon, the peacock, the crab,
and other animals that brought me gold and money?

I also yearn greatly for Samarkand and its weavers' quarters,
with those young Turks, who now appear in my daydreams.

I regret no longer being able to see my dear Sayyed Tegin,
although down here he says that he deeply hates our kinship.

I'm also nostalgic for those young donkeys that are now adult servants,
and dress themselves up so finely with my clothes and my turban.

Lastly, I am very depressed not to have my poems with me any more,
even if, as the fruit of my vile, rotten nature, they are cold and nasty.

I have only one wish, O poet: when you wake from this sweet dream,
I really implore you, do not spare your curses on me and my poems!'

So be it! A thousand curses on Nezâmi and his poems
will I write when I am awake and when I am asleep.

Afflicting that evil bastard in this way
is one of the few good deeds I can do.

I expect then a reward from Mojir od-Din,
he who is surely a great and noble person.[192] *Suzani*

One of the most argumentative characters in the whole of the literary history of Persia is Khâqâni, as demonstrated by the fact that he is a central figure in a dense network of conflicts and quarrels. Of the many satires he wrote against his colleagues, here are two about Vatvât:

This cat-eyed little brute, this poodle from Ghur, this dinky faggot,[193]
this hideous feeble creature, this tiny impotent being, this ugly pagan,

with me he tries to be a small panther, but is an undersized vixen,
a feeble sow-necked creature, a pooch with the nature of a jackal.

He claps his minute hands like a monkey and hops about like a bear,
this insignificant character with a goatee beard and baboonish looks.

He is a tiny hermaphrodite hare, both male and female,
menstruating like a woman and screwing like a midget.

He was my household pet and now, for my bad luck, he's become
a lion cub or, rather, a wolf cub. Indeed, he's a little worse than both.

That mangy hair of a dog, I refer to him as a dog's cock
because he peeks out bare and reddish like a dog's cock.

Like a cowardly small panther he runs after deer and jumps on them,
people endure him only because of love's talisman on his puny chest.

He wants to play the swaggering bully round the gazelles and fawns
at the king's feast, but remains an onager foal at his mummy's feet.

Like a doggy, he is a paragon of loyalty. This blithe little creature
will not even abandon someone who hammers his hands and feet.

He has no honour, like a tiny beaver with no balls,
this bad-tempered jackalette, this touchy little mule!

Khâqâni, don't moan! It is not even clear who this pooch belongs to!
This doggy, who only munches small bones, can easily be satisfied:

if he grunts a little bow-wow, you can simply throw him a few crumbs,
and, slightly wagging his tail, he will go to lie down behind a little door.

You, O Khâqâni, are the measure of wisdom, and must not be hurt
by this tiny scorpion who would like to sting you with his evil tail.

It was a similar blow that, after the month of Shavvâl,[194]
struck the blessed nape of the son of Toghân Yazak.[195] *Khâqâni*

That impotent fag is an owl standing on a dung heap,
and, unlike the Homâ, he vaunts no noble origins.[196]

He eats garbage and is as sinister as a crow,
like a rooster he is adulterous and depraved.

He's as mocking and brazen as a turtledove,
like a parrot he is a spy and a squealer.

He is really just as aggressive as an eagle,
like a great bird of ill omen, he elicits fear.

Unlike the sparrow-hawk he doesn't live in princely dwellings,
but always perches, with his tawny-owl face, on the battlements.

He has none of the nobility of the falcon or the fame of the phoenix,
but only the notoriety of the hoopoe and the nature of the vulture.

Like a wagtail he hops from branch to branch,
like a little bat he flaps from tavern to tavern.

Like the peacock he's the devil's eternal guide,
like the sparrow he is constantly fouling things.[197]

As long as Khâqâni is the nightingale of speech,
he will be stalled like a merlin on a windy day.

He became my enemy, I the white hawk,
and his fate turned as black as a crow.

O if only the king's sword were immediately
to split open his head, like a swallow's tail.[198] *Khâqâni*

Among the satirical attacks aimed at Khâqâni himself, there are significant lines by his master Abu 'l-'Alâ':[199]

O Khâqâni, although you know the art of speech,
I want to say something. Listen, it costs you nothing!

Don't make *hajv* on somebody older than yourself,
you might be talking to your father without knowing it.[200] *Abu 'l-'Alâ'*

Listen, Afzal od-Din, if you are asking me sincerely,
for your dear soul's sake, I'm dissatisfied with you!

In the whole region of Shervân you were famous[201]
as the carpenter's son. I gave you the title of Khâqâni!

I did numerous other good deeds for you:
I gave you my daughter, goods and fame.

Why do you fail to show me respect?
I was a father to you and I'm your master!

How long will you keep on with your insisting
that I said things of which I have no memory?

By God, I never said: 'I fucked you!'
And if said it, by God, I don't remember!

Not one, but two hundred times did I actually make a point of saying:
'I didn't fuck you, I didn't fuck you, I didn't fuck you, I didn't fuck you!'

But if you keep repeating that I said it, all right then:
'I fucked you, I fucked you, I fucked you, I fucked you!'[202] *Abu 'l-'Alâ'*

Khâqâni was also considered to be a target of his putative student Mojir od-Din in the following lines:

He's so depraved that his nature is a real disgrace to life,
his lust makes him thirsty even when he's sitting in water.

His soul would still be as black as the back of a mirror,
even if Alexander built his mirror from that black soul.[203]

With my ice-cold sigh I have prepared a talisman for good health,
so that, like a salamander, I can pass through the fire of his hate.

God made him a vain, odious hypocrite,
full of all kinds of flaws, short and all red.

No one knows him, but he claims to be a celestial pole for people.
He is surely a pole: the only thing near him is his daughter's coffin![204]

He cuts off his nose to spite his face, and I think
he does so to be compared to the carpenter's son.[205]

People actually refer to him as Abraham, the family-destroyer,
but only because Âzar of Shervân's son treats him like a brother.

But he must be exactly the opposite of Abraham,
otherwise why is the basil of my nature a fire to him?[206] *Mojir od-Din*

Other contemporary poets, such as Jamâl od-Din, also criticised Khâqâni:

Who will take my message to the city of Shervân?[207]
Who will take my words to that eloquent man?

Who will say to him: 'O Khâqâni, what on earth are all these boasts?
Writing two lines is not enough for you to adopt an illustrious title!'

You've claimed there is no one like you in the whole world,
saying your speech is superior to that of Qeys and Sahbân.[208]

A man of intellect does not show off his learning,
if he does, he must prove the truth of what he says.

A man with so little knowledge as you can lay no claims to erudition!
A man like you with no talent can't speak of himself and the great!

You sent us your poetry as a gift, a foolish action:
no one with any sense would carry cumin to Kerman![209]

You believe the wise and knowledge have abandoned our land,
otherwise how could someone like you make such huge claims?

The fact you send us poetry reminds me of the ant
who went to Solomon and gave him a locust's leg.[210]

You consider your words to be like a necklace made of pearls,
but if one wants to make money, would one carry pearls to Oman?

You may well think that your speech is a kind of white magic,
but no one dares to compare his own miracles to those of Moses.

An old woman on a donkey's back is an unpleasant sight,
especially when trying to gallop and race on a feast day.

Someone brought your poems to our land so as to boast about them.
If he had had some nous, he'd have given them to a straw merchant.

No wise man ties dogs to the mosque,
no Muslim takes idols into the Kaaba.

Perhaps your fellow citizens have never read poetry,
since they have notebooks and divans with your poetry.

In that country which is devoid of imagination,
those wretched poems are galloping horses.

But our land is not the kind of place where anyone
making one paltry poem, can claim to be like Tayyân.[211]

In our land there are still some poets
who hold eloquence in great honour.

I am one of them and, when I write poetry,
Hassân's soul bows down before my talent.[212] *Jamâl od-Din*

Mojir od-Din was another poet at the centre of a notorious controversy because of some poems that he had composed casting aspersions on the city of Isfahan.[213] For this reason he was the butt of Jamâl od-Din's satires:

O little Mojir, why on earth did you write that *hajv*?
Do you know what will happen to you for those lines?

You have used your terrible tongue against Isfahan,
and you can't imagine what trouble is on the way.

For how much longer will you say that the people of Isfahan
do not have any kind of talent for expressing refined subtleties?

If I tell cities like Ganja and Tbilisi to go and get fucked,
think what I can say to towns like Shervân and Beylaqân.[214]

If I can invoke a fart on the beard of the master Khâqâni,
just think what I can wish for a great cuckold like you.[215] *Jamâl od-Din*

From the outset when God, through grace and mercy,
created the reasoning spirit from the rays of Intellect,

Intellect set its nipples on the poets' mouths,
so that each sucked according to his skill.

Mojir od-Din arrived late, the milk had been finished,
so, into his gaping mouth, Intellect dropped a big turd.[216]

Jamâl od-Din

Rivalry between poets was not always characterised by such long dissertations. Sometimes we find pithy repartee, as in the following famous exchange between Adib Sâber and Vatvât:

That minuscule faggot Rashid-e Vatvât
is to ignorance what Hippocrates is to science.

If there were talk of cocks in hell,
he'd jump off the bridge of salvation.[217] *Adib Sâber*

That minuscule faggot Adib Sâber
made *hajv* on me for no reason.

So I am going to fill his mouth up with shit,
even though it's absurd to carry dates to Basra.[218] *Vatvât*

We end this survey of poetic rivalries *ad hominem* with a satire on Nezâmi-ye Ganjavi, which is interesting and curious, especially in the light of the moral prestige traditionally enjoyed by this poet. The satire is an extract from ʿÂref-e Ardabili's *Farhâdnâme*, a *masnavi* which, in some parts, may be considered a kind of obscene response to Nezâmi-ye Ganjavi's *Khosrow o Shirin*:

When Nezâmi's inspiration dimmed for ever,
he handed on his cup of sweet wine to me.

I ask pardon on behalf of that elderly master,
and I'll tell you, dear friends, how things stand.

In narrating Khosrow's life, in fact,
he did not say some crucial things.[219]

When he spoke of the kind deeds of that prince,
who was intent on piercing the virgin pearl of Shirin,

he failed to pay close attention to the deeds of Farhâd,
who' d already manfully taken what was due from Shirin.

Nezâmi believed it pointless to celebrate a foreigner
like Farhâd, given the great regal prestige of Khosrow.

Nezâmi always lived in his own city,
and never bothered about foreigners.

But I suffered the hardship of journeying,
having been forced to go far from home.

I have been confined to a lonely life in Shervân,[220]
with no friends, confidants, relatives or kinsmen.

That loneliness deeply affected my mind,
and from my inner self oil came for my lamp.

My heart went out because of Farhâd,
and the light of sympathy lit within me.

I decided therefore to start recounting his numerous deeds,
as a foreigner who felt compassion for a fellow foreigner.

What is certain for me was doubtful for Nezâmi,
and what for Nezâmi was obscure is clear to me.

Amorous games were not Nezâmi's line,
his mind, therefore, could not describe them.

How can a man who has never grasped the cup
go about describing the state of the drunkard?

Only the drinker of wine knows its purity!
Inebriety's music can only be heard by drunks!

I know for certain that, during his courtings,
Nezâmi never consummated a carnal relation.

He was not a heretical painter like Mâni,[221]
he was a man totally devoted to the spirit.

And anyone made wise by intellect
will be only strictly pure in love.

A person who has knowledge for a counsellor
will be detached from true amorous games.

He depicted the path of passion in such a way
that you would say had never been in love.

His manner of speaking made any kind of narrative monotonous,
in his moderation he didn't distinguish between man and woman.

He described in unsuitable tones love's happy time,
thus cooling completely the big flames of passion.

Men were stripped of all their virility in his words,
behaving like an old fellow, Nezâmi made love insipid.

Whereas, on the contrary, describing beautiful people
is our profession, and we have their features in our mind.

O my friend, whichever art you choose to learn,
remember that no one will master it like the experts!

Only someone who always keeps the company
of the drunken heart-breaker knows his mood.

I have experienced these stories first hand,
I have felt the mood of delicate beautiful boys.

I have also seen idols who were veiled whores,
celebrated by people because of their chastity:

behind their show of modesty and abstinence,
they were continually plotting how to deceive.

There are many secrets I could unveil,
I only need choose which to narrate.[222] *ʿÂref-e Ardabili*

At times the satire is addressed not to a particular poet but to a group of poets as the expression of a corrupt, incompetent class:

Having sufficiently celebrated the just,
I'll now speak about those who drivel.

They are people with neither skill nor vigour,
and are as useless as a cock with no balls.

Always inclined towards hypocrisy and deceit,
they measure the world for their own calculations.

They take their poems to those who wash or weave,
selling them for the price of a pair of shoes or a turban.

Like junk merchants, they make other people's old things new,
establishing the price of one of their poems at only two loaves.

They beg like hungry dogs from door to door,
and call the worst of poisons sweet delicacies.

They address *madh* to the rabble that should be for kings,
and they put their intellect at the service of the devil.

They are a herd of brazen idiots,
who use disgusting, ugly words.

They describe the crown as if they were referring to a chain,
their poetry has no strength, just as their cheeks have no beard.

None of them can express themselves properly,
and they are unable to tell right from wrong.

They don't know the difference between *tâbe* and *âftâbe*,[223]
they confuse the form of the sky with that of a comet,

for them *kâse* is the same as *korâse*,
and *tâs* is no different from *tâse*.[224]

They recite praises to the sovereign meant for governors,
and raise governors as high as the status of Mercury.[225]

They call ordinary folk lords,
and address nobles as servants.

Since they can't distinguish between praise and blame,
their houses and their wives' cunts are both wrecked.

They are always on the lookout for a morsel of bread,
but go round searching with no means and no wits.

Perpetually with dirty miserable faces,
they behave like scroungers and spies.

Their countenance and figure bring bad luck,
so they are perennially wretched and ruined.[226] *Sanâ'i*

Court Milieu

Collective satire is also aimed at social categories other than poets who are also in attendance at the court. Here are three examples. The first is a satire against physicians, the second concerns cup-bearers and singers and the third describes some notables:

Scientists have described symptoms in books,
small and large, of all the gravest diseases.

But if you ask the physicians of today
about only one of those symptoms,

I assure you they won't understand a thing,
even if they leaf through book after book.

Out of ignorance, they are always trumpeting on,
but are worse than dull dim-witted street-sweepers.

They are all so competent that every year
they kill thousands and thousands of patients.

They are mates with the angel of death,
assassins, and people are their victims.

Pity the poor wretches who require
such a category of brazen blind men.

O Lord, please free us, I beg You,
with Your grace, from such physicians!

The world is in ruins because of them,
save people from these wicked men![227] *Sanâ'i*

You may well relinquish the paradise of the beyond,
and abandon the realm of the world down here,

if you enjoy this banquet of joy and smiles:
even heaven will bow down before it.

The cup-bearers are like the moon and the host like the sun,
the wine is as strong as Mars, the singers as melodious as Venus.

Celebrated in every city, the singers
make Venus seem a modest apprentice.

Each has blown out from his arse
unforgettable angelic melodies.

Right from between their thighs, some air has risen
into lovers' instruments, and those cocks have swollen.

To seduce and to pretty themselves like half-moons,
they have dressed up with some fine double chins.

Meanwhile the cupbearers at that feast
are drunk with cup in hand and cock in feet.

Some are devoted to trials of love,
while others, all lust, are jerking off.

The shiest ones, with their swift movements,
have ended up under the axe of the strongest,

and even the abstinent are red-faced with joy,
their necks grown purple from slapping.[228] *Sanâ'i*

Heaven has bestowed significant court honours
on whomever I have stuck it up as far as the balls.

My pansy friends have become important,
while in their eyes I am still a nonentity.

Alas that not even only once
can I stick it up my own arse![229] *Suzani*

As in the cases of patrons and poets, the other social categories may also be attacked at the personal level. At times the name of the *mahju* is mentioned, as in this poem:

When Mohammad the flautist plays,
his flute has the power of an organ.

A breath is blown down that pipe,
and cheers up every heart full of grief.

Since his melody enlivens their souls,
people willingly give their heart to him.

What pleasure is to be had, when he so dexterously
invents fine games with that two-eyed instrument.

From his authority come orders and bans,
from his words flow gold and pearls.

He brings together all the musicians,
and raises the curtain on the stage.

Then the bald Nâser bustles to and fro,
advances amidst pushing and great blows.

That donkey with a wrecked arse
bangs a shameless cock-eating whore.

For him the aim of all this beating
and din is only to earn his bread.

That depraved wretch and that whore
are actually good at making us laugh:

that cuckold gets angry and huffy,
and at once slaps begin to fly all over.

He only has to see a crumb, even in rubbish,
and he's willing to sacrifice his whole house.

He loves money above all else,
that's why he's a true cuckold.[230] *Mas'ud-e Sa'd*

But the addressee more often remains anonymous, as in the following examples:

The judge is not well acquainted with me, otherwise he would give me,
at least, his fleas, passing them off as poppy and sesame seeds.

He is aware, however, that if I make the cock of *hejâ* hard,
his arse will start to fart, out of fearfulness, at every instant.

But, by God, he's so stingy he won't even give you a coriander grain,
no matter how much you threaten to lop off his head like a leek's.[231]
Qomri

That blood-letting Jew has evil pagan blood,
his tongue is slow but his scalpel's tip is fast.

I asked him to cut a slit in a vein as narrow as my cunt,
he paid no heed and made one as broad as his wife's arse.[232] *Mahsati*

In this context we have the significant cases of those beloved young craftsmen who are mocked within the framework of the genre called *shahrâshub* ('upsetting the town'). Their good looks are the cause of havoc in the town:

My handsome butcher skinned a tail,
held it up and said: 'What a beauty!'

I murmured to myself: 'What incredible greed!
With all the tails he has, he still loves a tail!'[233] *Mahsati*

Albeit rarely, the beloved may also be described in ironic terms outside any professional context. His haughtiness may be criticised:

Yesterday I caught sight of a beautiful boy at Zuzan,[234]
if you want to praise the beautiful, he's the one to praise.

He showed no pity for my heart and took a wife.
And that unfaithful wife avenged my heart on him.[235] *Mahsati*

The physical decline of the beloved also provides an opportunity to mock him:

As soon as your chin had a beard,
that beard was pointed at by all.

Your beard grew and then you tore it off. I am sure
that's what you did, otherwise where has it gone?[236] *Mahsati*

As we have seen on the subject of patrons, in the case of other categories the criticism may also be less concerned with daily life and take on more didactic and moralising tones. Here is an example concerning a general aspect of the court milieu, in which the intimate friends of the sovereign (represented by the falcon) are bundled with him in a negative judgement:

The falcon entered the banquet with haughty mien,
eagerly intent on disclosing some secret truths.

He started bragging about his privileges,
showing off the noble headgear he had.[237]

He said: 'Because of my passion for the king's hand,
I have closed my eyes on the people of the world.

Here's why I keep my head under this hood:
so my feet are always on my king's hand.

I carefully taught myself to behave properly,
following a discipline worthy of an ascetic,

so that I would know the rules of service
for when they took me to the king's court.

Why on earth should I dream of the Simorgh?[238]
Why should I so recklessly rush towards him?

I'm happy being fed with a few morsels from my king,
because being in this place is enough for me in the world!

I don't aspire to set off on a journey,
I'm proud to remain on my king's wrist.

He who is worthy of a king
will then have that king's ear.

That's why being worthy of him
is better than roaming endless valleys.

I intend to spend my whole life
joyfully down here with my king,

either waiting for him to come to me,
or hunting because of my love of him.'

The hoopoe replied: 'O prisoner of forms,
those forms are far from true qualities!

If a king has an equal in his kingdom,
what value can his realm have for him?

Power only pertains to the Simorgh,
he is the peerless king in the world.

He who foolishly puts a chief
in every land is no true king.

Only he who has no equals and lives
loyally and courteously is a true king.

The kings of this world may also be fair,
but sooner or later they commit tyranny.

The closer you are to them,
the darker your future will be:

you must always be on the alert with them,
your life is always in danger next to them.

The kings you see around you are like fire,
avoid them, it's the only way to live in peace!

They want no one around them,
so why go near them? Fly away!'[239] *'Attâr*

Religious Context

Other frequent targets for satire are the religious establishment and religious figures. The satires of this kind are usually generic rather than personal. Very few names are actually mentioned. The criticism may be serious and with no obscenities, as in the following example:

O *mufti*, we surely are much more serious than you,[240]
despite all our drunkenness, we are soberer than you!

We drink the blood of the vine, and you that of people.
Be fair: which of us must be considered more bloodthirsty?[241]
'Omar Khayyâm

Here are another two examples in this moderate style. The first is a ghazal aimed at the hypocrisy of preachers:

The preachers on the *menbar* and before the *mehrâb* behave properly,[242]
but when they retire on their own, they do other, very different things.

I have a question for the wise man who sits in the assembly:
'Why do those calling for repentance, then repent so little?'

You might say that they don't believe in Judgment Day,
given all the deceits and tricks they play on our Lord!

I bow before the Old Man of the Tavern: his dervishes[243]
have no needs and they cast dirt on all the world's riches.

O my great Lord take these parvenus back to their donkeys,
they brag too much about having Turkish slaves and cattle.

And you Angel, recite prayers at the door of love's tavern,
because that is where Adam's clay is kneaded and shaped.

Several lovers have already been slain by His infinite beauty,
but in love many new lovers always appear from nowhere.

O you who go begging at the house of the Sufi, stand up now!
At the convent of the Magi they offer water making hearts strong.

O my heart, empty your house and make of it a dwelling for the king,
these pleasure-seekers have made their heart and soul a battlefield.

At dawn voices came from the celestial throne, and the Mind said:
'You would think that the saints recite Hâfez's poetry from memory!'[244]

Hâfez

The second ghazal is aimed at the hypocrisy of the Sufis:

For God's sake don't hang around with those wearing the cowl,
and instead show your face to the libertines who own nothing.

The cowls they have hide a lot of filth,
hurrah for the clothes of the wine-seller!

You are of a sensitive nature and surely can't stand
the dullness of a handful of people dressed in tunics.

You can easily see what the deceit of those hypocrites leads to,
the jug has a bleeding heart and the lutes send out laments.

You got me drunk, now don't hide yourself away from me!
You gave me sweet nectar, now don't make me drink poison!

In those who pose as Sufis I have never seen any kind of suffering,
may the joy of those who drink wine to the last drop always be pure!

You should watch out for Hâfez's ardour,
he has a breast which is like a boiling pan.[245]

Hâfez

Unlike the last three poems, many of the satires in the religious context contain obscene language and imagery. Some are short and epigrammatic, like the following:

A sheikh said to a prostitute: 'You are drunk,
every instant you fall into a different trap.'

She replied: 'I am everything you say,
but are you in reality as you appear?'[246] *'Omar Khayyâm*

When that idol of pagan faith came to pray,
believers and dervishes interrupted the orations,

and the imam said, with great suffering and regret:
'If only he were in front of me and I behind him!'[247] *Sa'di*

At other times we have a sort of story with a plot and a moral at the end:

I've heard that in the city of Herat,
there was an erudite and skilful man.

Being tired because of the infinite suffering he saw all around,
he acquired so much learning that he was the wisest in the world.

His knowledge was incomparable,
but he was troubled by a vexation.

He had just one vexation and no other,
the vexation due to his cock's vigour.

He hadn't had a fuck for such a long time and when,
at last, he picked up a boy, he didn't know where to go.

Finding no other possible place, he was forced,
having no other choice, to go into the mosque.

Seeing there was no one in front of the *mehrâb*,[248]
he decided to have a quick fuck, there and then.

He drew down the veils from those silvery hills
so as to send his own fish back up to the spring,

and the mosque was flooded by such light
that a reflection flashed out from within.

A devout man was struck by that glow,
and set off to see what was going on.

From afar he noticed the boy bent double,
and a depraved man with his tool in his fist.

When, after entering, he slowly drew a bit closer,
he saw the man was slipping it up the boy's arse.

He began to wave his hands and to whirl a stick,
then, opening his mouth, he roared like a bull:

'You damned people are the only ones to blame
if there is no rain and the crops do not grow!

What effrontery is this in the holy dwelling?
The divine law certainly doesn't thrive in you!

What kind of behaviour do you think this is?
For the divine law, it's a disgrace and shame!

The end of the world really has finally come,
now it's the turn of ignorance and the ignorant!

No one holds God in fear any longer,
people's hearts are prey to temptation.

And on account of these kinds of evil actions,
there's no rain in the sky and the earth has no fruit.

If you commit the sins of sodomy and adultery,
then the eye of the Spring cloud will dry up,

all the plants will disappear from the world,
and people will lose their means of subsistence.

Creation will inevitably be destroyed,
when there is sodomy before the *mehrâb*.'

With a quick trick the depraved man jumped away,
so that he would not be caught by the devout man.

But no sooner was he out of the mosque door,
than the devout man took up the job, from the start.

And when the depraved man turned round,
to look at what the devout man was up to,

he saw the devout man had laid his carrot at the entrance
of the young boy's sack, without even offering a penny.

Sticking his head round the door, he said: 'O devout man,
this is the same mosque as before and that's the same boy.

Is our destiny so different and the situation changed so much
that everything prohibited for me is now legitimate for you?'

'God be praised!', replied the devout man,
'The things of the world have really changed:

the earth now has plants in abundance,
and people have a means of subsistence.

Thanks be to God! It would seem
that pearls, not rain, fall from the sky.

The clouds, once dry, are full of water,
and people's hearts have all cheered up.

The crops have grown vigorously again,
and the things of the world are back in place.'

O you, who fear God and always show pity and rightfulness,
O you, thanks to whose influence the world is in good health,

O you, who are so respectful of places of worship,
and may justifiably be described as a true Muslim!

If this is what the devout of the world are like,
what on earth can we expect from the others?

Run away from the house and from the street
of a devout man, a Sufi, who does such things!

And when a Sufi behaves like this,
a world of cocks up his wife's cunt!

It's true that these devout people exist,
they are as empty inside as cowbells.

Bound by the snares of hypocrisy and falsity,
what they really deserve is a hundred sneers.

Don't pay any attention to these kinds of Sufis
and their stories! Tell something about yourself!

They are the slaves of mindless fellows,
they humiliate themselves before people.

By dint of slappings may their necks
become like cotton in the dyer's hands![249] *Sanâ'i*

One place frequently associated in satirical terms with the depravation of religious people is the *khâneqâh* (Sufi monastery):

Hey khâje Sharaf, O you, who come from Herat,
and in a hundred ways have been a wife to believers!

You have suddenly become a sheikh yourself. What a pitiful sight!
You have become a master when no one expected it. What ignominy!

Your cell let out a moan and your prayer rug a sigh,
both are ashamed of you, so filthy and so impure.

May my fart shelter in the alcove of your beard,
and my cock take refuge in the hole in your behind!

Indeed, in what better cell than your arse
could I leave my one-eyed, bald club?

With all those hairs your arse is like a Sufi,
and with my cock it has found a fine turban.

If you set your arse for a short while on the prayer rug,
your brow will be blackened by the stink coming off it.[250]

Your eyes are sunk in the pit of your nose
to avoid seeing your ill-omened face.

Those eyes that remind anyone observing them
of mercury quivering at the bottom of a well.

You're like a dog and cat at the same time, but with monkey's face!
It's terrible that someone like you is in charge of such a *khâneqâh*![251]

Qomri

The *khâneqâh* is sometimes described as a place of pleasure where the confreres, led by particularly libidinous companions, give vent to their sexual instincts, as we read in the following lines:

The eye of a mystic's heart fell on a pretty face,
he saw those curls and they captured his mind:

he was a robust young man with impudent looks,
an expert at wrestling with chain-breaking brawn.

The mystic spent several days tempting that young man,
and eventually one night managed to be alone with him.

He put his hands on his musky apple,[252]
and kissed that sweet fruit several times.

Then he set about opening his breeches,
so he could plunge his arrow therein.

The young man was irascible and rough,
and threatened whippings and punches.

'I will never accept' he said 'such shame:
never will a free forehead rub on the ground!

But if kisses and hugs are all you want,
I am your slave, come and take them!'

The other replied: 'I agree to this pact,
O flourishing sapling and sinuous cypress!

Hugging you tight is really enough for me,
and to die at your feet, O my heart-breaker!'

They made their peace with these words,
and clasped each other in a long embrace.

They laid lip on lip, in love and agreement,
like two almonds in the interior of a shell.

The mystic keenly laid a hand on his beloved's neck,
his desire grew so strong his cock was about to burst.

All of a sudden he completely lost control,
got behind him and stuck it up his arse.

Patience was utterly defeated and passion prevailed,
he plunged in his banner, leaving only the handle outside.

The other said: 'What's this? Have you lost your head?
What a piece of cowardice, what a shameful thing!'

The mystic had now totally succumbed to his own desire,
and wouldn't let his friend so stupidly slip from his grasp.

So he dropped some coins into the beloved's fist,
hoping to win over that powerful arm with gold.

And that stunning boy let him in the back-shop,
saying: 'Stick your nail as far up as it will go!'

The mystic felt great joy and satisfaction,
for all his coming and going in there.

He took the young man to his friends and mates,
and left him to stay with the other confreres.

Some of them gave him a little kiss,
others a bougie up to his umbilicus.

Some showed all their fondness for him,
others offered him friendship and devotion.

But then they all began to fight over him,
and their yelling reached as high as the sky.

Screams, slaps and eventually stones began to fly,
and every confrere ended up with a bruised face.

So they went to their old Master,
and they told him the whole story.

He bent his head, soon began to reflect,
and, raising his face, proffered his counsel:

'For people who usually survive only by begging,
one pair of sandals must suffice for twenty feet!'

These words were so welcome to all,
they were like a salve on a throbbing sore.

They set about prostrating themselves,
chanted poems and clapped their hands.

No one had ever put that young wrestler on his back,
but now all of them pressed his forehead to the ground.

That tulip face began to be inebriated with them,
he took lots of cocks until his beard started growing.

Only then did he give up, imploring forgiveness:
such poor wretches must always be very patient![253] *Sa'di*

We also find detailed descriptions of the general decadence in the *khâneqâh*, especially in terms of the circumstances leading to the corruption of young adepts by false masters:

In the past people were honourable,
and usually had courteous manners.

Today there's no trace of those people or manners,
no one bothers to even make mention of them.

Everywhere you find a traitor making traps,
and laying down his snares of deception.

He sits in the place of honour saying: 'I am the sheikh!',
while several boys like full moons stand all around him.

He seems to be painted there in his *khâneqâh*, stuck in like a nail,
but only because he's a wretch and doesn't know where else to go.

He preens away at his moustache and beard,
and hides bottles and hashish under his cushion.

He has chosen some despicable types in the city,
and keeps them all lined up in a row next to him.

They are a debauched band with wrecked arses,
people who have never listened to the masters.

They all have their tools straight and ready,
at the continual thought of their beloveds.

During the day they work hard without eating or sleeping,
at night they take loads of money to that place of pleasure.

All that they earn in three days' work,
they blow in an instant with their beloveds.

Those debauched men have their heartbreakers in there,
and are like wolves prowling round so many Josephs.[254]

Some of them bring fruit and yogurt,
and prepare everything for the night feast.

That *khâneqâh* is crammed full with cupboards,
bows, backgammon, chess and carafes of iced water.

The table abounds with loaves and pans brimming with food,
while all the bodies and hearts are stripped of humanity.

They shove at each other, fighting and joking,
not heeding the motion of the stars and heaven.

To take advantage of handsome boys,
a rumour is put about in their city:

'A brother, more generous than anyone else,
has just opened the doors of his *khâneqâh*!

There you will find a table that is overflowing with sweet syrups,
you can hear stories, dance and be with companions and masters,

there you can crack the rod on iron hoops,
get exercise with weights and javelins,

use long arrows, gloves, slings
and other similar instruments.'

With these words they deceive the boys' fathers,
profit from their ignorance and bury the boys alive.

Those fathers are stupid and their sons are simpletons,
that's why the debauched men can satisfy their own desires.

Why should those boys put up with the rigours of the family,
when they can be pampered in that fashion down there?

It would be silly to go back home,
hear all those counsels and tirades,

endure the torments of their fathers and masters,
see food only from afar and have to do housework,

leaving the witticisms, games and jokes,
all those delicacies, lawns and gardens.

If one were by nature lively and quick,
bright, intrepid, well-balanced and upright,

seeing there was no virtue to be learned,
or perfection and nobility to be acquired,

he would never become the laughing-stock
of that host, only for some raisins and nuts.

But those idle good-for-nothings, those sweet-eating cowards,
wouldn't leave that place, even if you shot an arrow at them.

Moreover, the big-whiskered fellows who gather there
describe those boys as a divine gift sent by Providence,

making them strike a pact for various presents:
one, for example, offers a bow and another a belt.

They praise those boys even if they commit deplorable actions,
and consider each of their faults as being the same as virtue.

All spend the night light-hearted and carefree,
never closing their eyes, always feasting away.

When day comes, all activities cease.
With the table bare and the host asleep,

each goes back to his own affairs,
thinking how to procure fresh victims.

When night comes again, it's back to those games,
and the chance for more pleasure and wasting.

So time passes, and the beardless youths
in that place never listen to anyone's advice.

But suddenly beards begins to dim their faces
and ruin the splendour of their former beauty.

The tulips vanish out of their gardens,
and freshness fades from their apple cheeks.

If they look for meat dishes, they won't get even a bowl of yogurt,
if they want some water, they will have to fetch it themselves.

They are always chased away, like dogs into the forest,
their fathers can't help them, and they don't have a trade.

At every instant their hearts grow darker and sad,
because of their flippancy the game is up for them.

Not even the whiff of any good has reached them,
they've drunk poison and will find no antidote.

Out of ignorance they have hurt themselves,
poor wretches, they have fucked themselves![255] *Owhadi*

In the following poem the accent is on the sheikh in charge of the *khâneqâh* and his illegal and depraved dealings with occasional guests welcomed from nearby cities:

Beware of the Sufis of these places and times,
they are all cowards and all great exploiters.

Whatever you trust them with they steal,
and they do whatever enters their head.

Their only activities are sleeping and eating,
none remember that one day they will die.

All they dream of are the table and soups,
their thoughts are only for their bellies.

For a home each has chosen
a *khâneqâh* or similar place.

To satisfy their desires and passions,
they have pans and kitchenware.

They lay down elegant carpets,
and set fine vases here and there.

They have the tripod up with a pan on the go,
and all the cooking utensils ready to be used,

always awaiting generous people,
who come from towns and cities,

to bring them a nice bit of meat or flour,
and thus be welcomed at their table.

Then, opening their bag of bragging,
they begin to say silly things to everyone.

They go on repeating drivel and nonsense
until they see that the soup is cooked.

Only when they see it about to be served
do they begin to look after their friends.

But they are only capable of being intimate with the soup,
and their eyes light up at the sight of the fire under the pan.

When a corrupt man gets the chance
to take a young lad out of the city,

he soon begins to think about these sheikhs,
and is ready to prostrate himself at their feet.

It thus happened that a man with a tablecloth full of bread,
dates wrapped in a rag, a bag of sweetmeats and a jar of halva,

came from the city, followed by an eager lad,
to visit the *khâneqâh* of one of these sheikhs.

He went inside and said: 'Hello!
I wish I could always live with you!'

The sheikh stood up and answered:
'To you my salutations and my respects!'

The two hypocrites embraced each other,
kissing each other's hands and hugging.

Then the lad also ran up and greeted the sheikh,
rubbing his face on the sheikh's hands and feet.

With Muslim piety the sheikh
kissed him on the forehead.

The sheikh went to sit in his place,
and began to ask about this and that:

how it was they were, what they were doing,
and inquiring after their families and goods.

He listened carefully to the answers one by one,
and then looked at the man of the two and asked:

'Is this boy here your son?
Or is a relative or a pupil?'

'None of these three', replied the other,
'but we have a very close relationship.'

And he spoke about remote connections,
thus making clear the secret of his story.

Anecdote

Amazed, a man once asked somebody:
'What bond do you have with that person?'

'He is a Turk and I am a Persian', replied the other,
'but we are very close indeed, almost relatives.

He has a garden full of trees,
and in one a crow made its nest.

Whenever the crow begins to sing,
its voice reaches my house here,

and, as long as I am in this house,
I'll hear the sound of that song.'

The story continues

After they had gone on talking for a while,
those two presented some food as a gift.

The sheikh rubbed his hands, sat down,
and promptly grasped the bread and halva.

He ate some things and put other things aside,
even taking the share of those who were absent.

Examining the sweetmeats and dates,
he chose some that he would eat at night.

He said prayers for those two generous men,
before going on to deal with erudite matters.

He then read a *tafsir* and a *hadis*,[256]
and spoke of the evil demon's tricks.

He didn't stop even for a minute to argue,
and ended up talking of other sheikhs.

He said a little about his own master,
and after that about other old masters.

He described in detail the miracles of one,
illustrated the spiritual heights of another,

and narrated a lot of polished and elegant stories,
but never went from the skin to the core of things.

If you yourself are devoid of passion and rapture,
how can you speak of others' passion and rapture?

That sheikh was not inspired by such feelings,
and it was no use his saying that others were.

Anecdote

Once in a village a gypsy said to his son:
'There's nothing better than a wheat loaf!'

His son asked him: 'Have you ever tried it?'
'No!', replied the other, 'I've never eaten it!

But I had an old great grandfather,
who, having been blessed by destiny,

long ago had seen, just outside the city,
someone who had tasted a wheat loaf.'

The story continues

The sheikh went on talking the hours away,
and with various expedients spoke till evening.

After a while he took some herbs that were in the store,
gifts from people who had come on previous occasions,

and prepared a few bowls of food,
to be offered to the guests for dinner.

The soup having been quickly eaten,
the bowls were all cleared away.

Lastly, the sheikh offered the sweets he had set aside,
and picked at them while telling some nice stories.

When most of the night had already gone by, the sheikh
thanked the two friends for their sweets and company,

and went off towards his bed chamber,
leaving that wolf alone with that lamb.

Naturally, left all alone beside such a famished wolf,
the defenceless lamb couldn't have come off unscathed.

The sheikh fell asleep but the depraved man stayed awake;
while the former rested, the latter immediately set to work.

In the shelter of that shameful sheikh's monastery,
the other man had his way just as he had wished!

Now, if you deplore that husband of a whore,
you might be told: 'Some suspicion is a sin!'[257]

But God says: 'Some suspicion', thus not all!
There are suspicions which are well founded!

These are not the things of Sufis and free men,
but trickery and the customary ways of pimps.

And if I used the name of sheikh and Sufi,
I beg to be forgiven for that big mistake.

What right has that cowardly Sufi
to be acknowledged with such titles?

It's shameful to give attributes and names
worthy of a sovereign to such deceivers.

When someone behaves in that way,
even the letters in his name are ashamed.

O, if only he had been an example
that could be held up to people![258] *Jâmi*

Not just corruption but also other negative aspects of religious circles are highlighted, such as the ignorance and superficiality of pilgrims:

The pilgrims have returned amidst great ceremonies,
full of sincere gratitude for the pity of merciful God.

They have endured the trials and tribulations in the holy places,
and now they are safe from hell and its painful punishments.

All of them have gone to Mecca from Mount ʿArafât,
and reverently said the canonical: 'I'm ready to obey You.'

They completed the pilgrimage and its rites,
and have come back home safe and sound.

I went out to welcome them,
something I'm not used to doing.

I went there because, in that caravan,
I had a dear, good and devoted friend.

I then turned to him and asked: 'So, tell me,
how did you survive this tough, fearful journey?

Since you went away and left me,
I have been in a state of sadness.

But now I am happy that you have undertaken
the pilgrimage, you really are unique in the world.

Well, how did you worship
that great and noble sanctuary?[259]

When saying your vows of renunciation,
what kind of intentions did you express?

Did you deny yourself everything,
with the exception of everlasting God?'

'No!', he replied. I asked him: 'Did you declare:
"I am ready to obey You willingly and reverently"?

Did you hear the call of God clearly,
and did you respond as Moses did?'

'No!', he replied. I asked him: 'When you stopped
on Mount 'Arafât and enjoyed that huge privilege,

coming to know Truth and denying yourself,
did you feel the breath of true knowledge?'

'No!', he replied. I asked him: 'When you slew
the lamb in the name of the wealthy and the poor,

did you see your base, vile soul,
and did you slay and sacrifice it?'

'No!', he replied. I asked him: 'When you entered
the sanctuary, did you feel like those in the cave,[260]

safe from the evil of your flesh and well protected
from the pain of separation and the punishment of hell?'

'No!', he replied. I asked him: 'Throwing
the ritual stones against the cursed devil,

did you cast completely out from yourself
all your evil habits and deplorable actions?'

'No!', he replied. I asked him: 'Standing
before the place where Abraham stood,

did you entrust your inner self to God,
with sincerity, faith and certainty?'

'No!', he replied. I asked him: 'When you went
on the circumambulation and trotted like an ostrich,

did you think of the circle of all angels
gathered round the Supreme Throne?'

'No!', he replied. I asked him: 'When you finished
the ritual run that goes from Safâ up to Marwa,

did you contemplate the two worlds in your purity?
Was your heart liberated from the hell of lust?'

'No!', he replied. I asked him: 'Before coming back,
with the pain of separation from the Kaaba in your heart,

did you bury yourself there,
did you become a putrid corpse?'

'Of everything you have just said', he replied,
'I didn't know what was right and what was wrong.'

'Well, my friend', I finally affirmed, 'you did not go
on the pilgrimage, you did not achieve your annihilation.

You simply went to Mecca, visited it and came back,
paying vast sums for the journey through the desert.

If you want to go on the pilgrimage,
follow the indications I have given you.'[261] *Nâser-e Khosrow*

Religious satire may occasionally even take on confessional tones, as in the following lines expounding an outrageous point of view on the leaders of the four principal juridical-religious schools of Sunnism:

Shâfe'i decreed that the game of chess is completely lawful,
and the imam says only what is right. Don't try and cheat!

Bu Hanife claims something even better about wine:
'Boil it up, and it will become a licit drink for you!'

And Ebn-e Hanbal says: 'If your are in pain,
take some drugs and have a good time!'

Lastly, if you listen to Mâlek, the fourth jurist,
he'll advise you to go with a young male slave.

Gamble, then, drink, take drugs and have a screw,
that's true faith according to these four imams.[262] *Nâser-e Khosrow*

Finally, there are cases when the religious feeling itself is called into question and the chosen victim is the Creator:

The All-knowing created and made nature beautiful.
But why did he forge it so full of flaws and faults?

If He made a good job of it, why ruin it?
And if He made a bad job, who is to blame?[263] *'Omar Khayyâm*

Women as Habitual Subject for Satire

Women are another target for satire in that society. There are general complaints about them:

Not just one woman but one thousand women
can't be trusted when it comes to making promises.

When fidelity and its pledges were conceived,
that idea was suspended on reaching women.

A woman will be your friend, but only
as long as she has no one else to love her.

When she finds the arms of another,
she will no longer wish to see you.

Woman is more inclined to passions than man,
but they are all passions to satisfy only herself.

When playing her games she always cheats,
her every deed is founded on hypocrisy.

Women often inflict suffering,
and never once are faithful.

If a man insists on putting them to the test,
he surely behaves even worse than they do.

A woman is the centre of deceit:
outside is all peace, inside is all war.

If she's your enemy, it's the worst disgrace in the world,
if she's your friend, it will mean the perdition of your soul.

If you tell her to do something, she won't even try to listen,
if you forbid her something, she'll go out of her way to do it.

If you are distressed, she'll be happy,
when you're content, she'll be in agony.

This is what the best of women do,
evil women's plotting is worse by far![264] *Nezâmi-ye Ganjavi*

When it comes to satirising women, however, their sexual desire is the main target for offence:

One day some noble women
went out to walk in the country.

Lingering a little out there,
they saw some donkeys grazing.

A jackass was lusting after a she-ass,
just as a lover desires his beloved,

and, with an ebony rod two metres long,
he began to shag as only donkeys know how.

That jackass kept pushing it in and out,
farting and braying with all his might.

Viewing that scene from afar,
one of the women sighed and said:

'O sisters, this is what it really means to get a cock!
This is surely what it really means to give your arse!

If fucking is what this donkey is doing here,
then our husbands only ever piss in our cunts!'[265] *Anvari*

Women, in fact, are often described as being of easy virtue:

O dissolute woman, your deed was secret,
but now can you conceal that bastard son?[266] *Rudaki*

She still keeps her cunt sealed very tight for you,
but she is a two-doored caravanserai for others![267] *Labibi*

O brother, if your beautiful wife
got with child while you were away,

there is no need for you to be suspicious of her:
an able hen can lay eggs even without a rooster![268] *Shatranji*

Because of immoderate erotic activity, the female organ is described in abnormal terms:

Look at his bride's vagina and vulva, her shoes and bag:
the first two are misshapen and the other two totally round.

The blame must be laid with no one but her,
because she has battered all four of them:

the first two panting flat on her back,
the other two slinking about sensuously.[269] *Labibi*

It's for my cock that you make the point of your curls like a *jim*,
and, with a smile, you shape your lips into a form similar to a *mim*![270]

You have made my cock so fresh with your beauty!
But your cunt is no use to it unless you sew it half up![271] *Ebn-e Khatib*

If your bag weren't as lean as your flanks,
when would you ever lust after others?

You have a slender mouth and big wide cunt.
O if only your cunt were like your mouth![272] *Qamar*

Among the negative inclinations attributed to women, there is also the desire for members of their own sex:

Here they are, the Baghdad women,
all dead keen to give it a good rub.

They have silver mortars and crush saffron in them,
and they don't feel the need to wield the heavy pestle.

They have little crystal boxes strewn with silver,
which, every two weeks, welcome red rubies.

They have silver caves with grassy surroundings,
and, right through the middle, a lively spring flows.

Those women roll round in twos, one on top of the other,
always together like a conjunction of stars in the sky.

Behind they have four silver cushions,
and in front they wear two silk bands.

When they rub on each other,
their moans reach up to the sky.

It's a roll on drums, not a banging of cunts!
And the whole world can clearly hear the din.

Hey brother, don't delay, be quick,
have a wank when you see such things!

The honour of the cock has gone with its luck,
since they raised their standard in such a way.

But come on, Khâqâni, what is this joking?
You know that jokes always end in tears.

If you stoop to speak about women,
you'll suffer the same harm as them.[273] *Khâqâni*

Irony about women is also expressed, in a sexual context, by resorting to descriptions of a frequent abuse, namely, sodomy. Sodomy of women is considered an integral part of masculine rights and any protests by women are mocked:

Seeing a jackass mount a she-ass,
our lady soon became quite randy.

In the middle of the night she hung above her husband,
on top of his rod, but then it slipped up her behind.

She said to him: 'Pull that horse out, it's the wrong road,'
but he replied: 'He won't budge, he's gone completely wild!'[274] *Mahsati*

A similar situation is illustrated at greater length in the following passage, in which the sodomy of a wife is given the blessing of a judge and, in the final line, even of the poet himself:

For people who might not have heard anything about it,
here is the story of the judge, the woman and the sodomite.

One day a little woman, who had a bugger for a husband,
went to a judge to try and free herself from that disgrace.

She turned to the judge and told her story:
'You, who settle rows between people,

I am a pure woman with a wicked husband,
who torments me by day and by night.

How is it that with the door open and the hall tidy,
he always wants to come in through the roof?'

The judge answered: 'Since the house is his,
he can choose whichever entrance he likes!'

Then that poor woman, overcome by shame, said:
'O just man, that ugly pervert does illicit things!'

And she continued: 'He eats bread from the back of the tray!'
The judge replied: 'There's no harm in turning a tray round!'

She insisted: 'He is always going up the hill!'
The judge exclaimed: 'He only goes up it to pray!'

Finally, the woman said: 'O Muslim, he sticks
his bastard cock up my arse and vexes me greatly!'

The judge grew grim and, irritated, said to the woman:
'You're mad, where else would you want him to put it?

What on earth does licit and illicit mean?
A good wife must satisfy her husband!'

That fair, even-handed, pious, devout judge
issued a truly appropriate sentence in this case.

The arse is the place for the cock by decree of Suzani:
women should stay at home and lift their buttocks up![275] *Suzani*

Satirising Members of a Family

The family is another of the social components targeted by poets' satire. In this sense the ninth book of *Hadiqat ol-Haqiqe* by Sanâ'i is emblematic, with its mocking of various types of relatives. The following description of a sister and a brother-in-law comes from that work:

Who on earth is this? It's your brother-in-law,
and his cock is nice and swollen for his wife.

He is always coming in and out of your house,
whether you like it or not, he's now family for you.

Everybody everywhere knows who he is:
he is the man who fucks your dear sister!

But he only fucks her when he gets gold,
only then does that jackass burst her cunt.

And when he doesn't get any money,
he sells that cunt to bulls and donkeys.

She gives him everything to get his cock,
but that dirty wretch is never satisfied.

And if she has problems paying him,
he threatens to leave her and to part.

For many years he has been fucking her for money,
but if the money stops coming, he'll kick her out.

A curse on your sister and your brother-in-law,
no one here can be happy on account of them.

Every time she wants to have a fuck,
she has to pay all her money to him.

If your brother-in-law gets no reward,
he won't split her cunt in two any more.

Alas that he who fucks your sister
is only waiting for your father to die.

O brother, may sisters and daughters
stay away from you, even if they're coy.[276]

Sanâ'i

The general negative remarks about relatives are also characterised by that embarassing flatus we have already seen as being typical of invective:

> Once I heard a story about the devil,
> who one day farted three thousand times.
>
> A man asked him: 'What happened?
> Why have you made all this wind?'
>
> The devil replied: 'Thousand farts are for the beard
> of him who gives his goods to his son and son-in-law:
>
> that wretched fellow must then beg
> and weep to get something to live on.
>
> The second thousand farts are for the beard
> of him who suffers in order to hoard money:
>
> he doesn't enjoy his goods or let them be enjoyed,
> he is ruined, but his heir is fine and prosperous.
>
> And may the last thousand farts
> also be in the beards of those two.'[277] *Ebn-e Yamin*

In some cases the mocked relatives are given more personal features and appear to be individuals known to the poet:

> Your father was a pious and principled man,
> he didn't have an unworthy nature like you.
>
> And your little mother never fornicated with anyone!
> Hey, may your head be in the arse of your father's wife!
>
> If your father keeps on saying that you are my son,
> a donkey's cock in the cunt of your father's wife![278] *Sanâ'i*

Offensive poetry is also aimed at relatives in the author's family. Here are three examples, about the poet's father, wife and son:

> For a father I have this great cuckold,
> that the world's Lord created from fire.

He is a twin of Âzar and Nimrod's companion,
and he has Joseph the carpenter as his master.[279]

His nature is as sharp as an axe,
his nature is as cutting as a saw.

During the day he's always arguing with heaven,
and at night he's always fighting with Saturn.

If Mars had been in the first sphere,
he'd have pierced it with two nails.

His heavy feet are all swollen,
and his empty skull has grown bald.

The flesh of his carcass is putrid
like cotton in an old ink-well.

He lost the sap from his face and the air swelling his head,
since the sap and air are now in his most precious member.

My poor mother had to flee to the *menbar*[280]
because of my father's merciless minaret.

Although I'm the best son of the age,
he's ashamed of my learning and intelligence.

Oh, if only Khâqâni had been a weaver,
and so could have avoided these words!

Although my soul and heart suffer
and are destroyed by his rough speech,

he is God's delegate for my daily bread.
O Lord, save him, then, from calamities![281] *Khâqâni*

Anvari has chosen a terrible whore for a wife,
because of her, all men on earth are adulterers.

As long as the world lasts, may her cunt be full of cocks!
But alas what a great pity that this world is so transitory![282] *Anvari*

Anvari doesn't fuck his wife
for fear she'll give birth to a son,

and that son, as soon as his father meets his death,
will take to dressing up pretty like modern boys.

Anvari's fear is that a benefactor, just like himself, will appear,
then get behind his son, stretch out his hand to caress his face,

and use all fine manners, like a father,
until he pulls down the pants of the boy,

and sticks the cock right into his arse,
forcing it up and down in the usual way.

Why should you give your soul for your son
only for someone to come and fuck him for free?[283] *Anvari*

There are also several 'self-satires', that is, poems written by the poet against himself. They are often obscene, and linked to sexual incapacity or impotence:

Last night I met a fine idol and, with great lust,
said to myself: 'Tonight I'll screw till I drop.'

But my member fell into a deep slumber,
and I didn't know what remedy to devise.

I said to him: 'If you can invent some kind of way
to make it hard, and put it in the bag of your behind,

I guarantee that then you will surely get
what you deserve from my generous nature.'

He answered, saying: 'Do you take me for Moses,
able to turn your stick into a snake by holding it?[284]

What do you want of me? I'm certainly not
Jesus, who was able to resuscitate the dead!'[285] *Mas'ud-e Sa'd*

Peoples and Towns

It is also common to find satires of a geographical and political nature aimed at certain peoples or a town's inhabitants. These satires represent one of the collective variants of the satirical *shahrâshub* genre:[286]

As long as the country is in the hands
of the Turks, free men will have no bread.

Try and be someone with a wrecked arse,
since this age is an age of wrecked arses.[287] *Kâferak*

Do you know why the inhabitants
of Ghazna liken their city to a sea?

Pearls lie hidden on the sea bed,
and shit and garbage float on top.

Well, what you see today in Ghazna are shits,
and those underground are the precious pearls.[288] *Anvari*

I thought that relief could come to the soul from Isfahan,
and that magnanimity was a ruby to be found in that mine.

I would never have thought that the inhabitants of Isfahan
were blind, with all the collyrium that's produced in that city![289]
Mojir od-Din

O Khâqâni, don't expect any loyalty from the inhabitants
of Baghdad, you won't find that elixir in a city of swindlers.

Even if the blood of the world flowed like the Tigris,
no one would shed even a single tear in Baghdad.[290] *Khâqâni*

At times an individual is singled out from the inhabitants of a city to symbolise its negative features:

It is said that the people of Qazvin are stupid,
and Najm of Qazvin is the living proof of it.

Yesterday a respectable man told me something
which confirms a similar idea about that hypocrite.

Our dear fellow Najm of Qazvin,
always speaks of himself as of a god.

But his house is as narrow and dim as a pagan's grave,
with a roof which is as dilapidated as the devil's den.

The portico is like the mouth of a fierce but debilitated dragon,
while the bedroom is shut tight like the tomb of deceitful sophists.

When he goes to lie down, he rests on seventy quilts:
his cushions, one on top of each other, add up to a ton.

At home he often sits face to face with a dear friend,
they worship each other like the idol and the idolater.

If one whispers on the other's whiskers: 'You are the best of our age!',
the other immediately replies in his ear: 'You are the glory of our time!'

If someone asks Najm of Qazvin who taught
the prophet to write, he jumps up and cries: 'Me!'

And if someone else asks him who wrote the important texts
of medicine, the old hypocrite says to his son in Turkish: 'You!'

If the masters are like these two great men described here,
may the beard of all the masters be up my arse to their chin![291]

Asir od-Din-e Akhsikati

Addressees with no Social Labels

The satirical poetry we have considered so far has been aimed either at individual representatives of social categories and groups (sovereigns, poets, professionals, craftsmen, clerics, women, relatives and peoples) or has involved those same categories and groups seen as collective wholes. There also exists a series of satirical compositions on individuals for whom no social labels have been given, or at least cannot be reconstructed today. At times only the names of these individuals are mentioned and little else, as in the following passage, in which the victim is described as being prey to an unbridled desire whose object is clearly unattainable:

Sahlân Rostam has earnestly sworn
he'll fuck all those whom I've fucked.

But how can he fuck his mother and sister?
He would certainly be sentenced to death.

And even if he fucks them, claiming
that a promise should always be kept,

he certainly cannot fuck himself,
unless he has more science than us![292] *Anvari*

Another two examples of this type appear to be particularly significant. The first, with an idyllic final hemistich providing a startling contrast to the harsher tones of the overall text, tells of the poet's anger at having lost a female slave to a certain Oghol, identified only by caricature, insults and curses:[293]

Hey, sun of the kingdom, late on last night
I was sleeping absent-mindedly, my wits gone.

In the morning, when I opened my eyes, I noticed
some people in our quarter. Like angelic messengers,

they said to me: 'Yesterday evening the world's sovereign
gave a woman, from among all your slaves, as a gift to Oghol.'

Divine commands and royal orders must be executed,
I am a compliant servant who obeys without protesting.

But it is truly insulting to leave, beside that dog,
a cypress with a starry face, a sun in a tulip's clothes.

He is a man who is ready to give away his wife for money.
Could our women be suitable for one who sells his wife?

Can someone who has been quietly fucked
by a hundred pansies ever be a bridegroom?

His mouth gapes from one ear to the other,
just like the mouth of a fish gasping in sewage.

His lips are like a Magus' buttocks, his ears are fans,[294]
he has the face of a demon and a big pot for an arse.

Hey you, whose arse is more worn than the devil's shoes,
have you found no other victim in the city except us?

No woman has an arse anything like yours,
going from head to foot, from heel to ear.

Until your beard turned white, you had a man,
why do you scream for want of women today?

Only now that your arse, having been bunged so often,
is worn and sore, you want a cunt. Try to be a little patient!

All the men in this world have stamped
brands on your arse from their cocks.

You are a servant from my stables, as impure as a hundred dogs,
but the dog of a whore-monger is really much better than you.

Your mother and all the little women in your family are whores,
listen to what I have to say and, just like a dog, try to pay heed:

may your wife always be in the arms of my son,
as long as violets, irises and primroses bloom.[295] *ʿAmʿaq*

The second example begins with a long, expertly scurrilous description (a full thirty-eight lines beginning with the word 'fart'). The reason for the poet's irritation is a series of wicked actions and, in particular, the theft of some barley belonging to the poet by a bigwig from Mazdaqân (in the north-west of Isfahan), identified only by the name Ziyâʾ and characterised by his evil behaviour and malevolent influence:

A fart whose thunder torments the celestial spheres,
a fart sorely vexing and annoying the whole world.

A fart that, should the trumpet of the universal judgment
blow as strongly, would have all the dead shitting for fear.

A fart that, if the hole is open below,
leaves a deep mark even on granite.

A fart that, if it lets off its fragrance under the sky's robe,
is so powerful it makes blood flow from Saturn's nose.

A fart whose roar clearly illustrates
the secret of living beings' cavities.

A fart that magically splits the hairs on a chin in two,
at a gathering where the most cutting tongues compete.

A fart that, if the lofty peak of a mountain got only a whiff of it,
the slopes of the mountain would be as full of holes as a rat's nest.

A fart that, if it were to let rip in Spring,
would jaundice the cheeks of the Judas tree.

A fart that, with a simple gust of its fragrant breeze,
makes sober people roll on the ground like drunks.

A fart that, like a falling star, shoots
and marks the dark night's long beard.

A fart that, like a whirlwind, rises into the sky,
transforming the Milky Way into a shitty way.

A fart that scatters the bright moon's halo like a blown crop,
if it unleashes even only one blast into the celestial vault.

A fart that, if it blows on the sun and moon,
puts out those two lamps in the firmament.

A fart that, even when it's a quiet one,
rumbles as loud as a peal of thunder.

A fart that, if it finds its way up the earth's nose,
stinks so much it rips every veil of the sky's nostrils.

A fart that, like dawn's arrow,
easily pierces the sky's shield.

A fart that, if it leaves for India,
raises perilous storms at sea.

A fart that breaks all the moorings
of the ship in whose sails it blows.

A fart that, if it sees a thick beard,
immediately nests in it like a hen.

A fart that, when it starts to play its sweet tune
in the morning, makes the dawn tear at its shirt.[296]

A fart that, like a flash of lightning,
uproots every old beard it grasps.

A fart that, if a drummer hears its sound,
he will be angry with the band's trumpets.

A fart that, if it handed over its reins to the morning breeze,
would allow the dung-beetle to enjoy the rose and the garden.

A fart that, if it goes through the garden,
makes a wet gherkin grow on a plane tree.[297]

A fart that, if it suddenly roamed around China,
would turn the musk deer's pouch into a dog's arse.[298]

A fart that, if at any time it were to enter into conjunction
with the sky's nostrils, would blind all the eyes of the stars.

A fart that lasts for such a long time
that the earth and the sky hold their nose.

A fart that is like a torrid high wind,
making your hair fall out with one touch.

A fart that tinkles in the celestial basin,
a fart of whose wind Venus' flute moans.

A fart that flutters about more than a pigeon in love,
a fart that soars so high it makes an eagle look like a hen.

A fart that, if it gets under someone's whiskers,
will fill up his mouth with heavy loads of shit.

A fart that, when it blows on a chin's fresh down,
will instantly make it fall out like Autumn leaves.

A fart that makes every beard it reaches
immediately long for the sharp razor.

A fart that, if a jackass happens to hear it,
he'll be so ashamed he'll never bray again.

A fart that produces, free of charge,
the fragrance of shit for the stupid.

A fart that, as soon as it comes out of its private meanders,
goes to give public audience on the beard of I know who.

A fart that, when it wants to go from Isfahan to Mazdaqân,
begins by blowing at the gates of the town of Guzdân.[299]

May a fart as I have described and another thousand like it
strike the beard of anybody wishing to be an enemy of poets.

Only that bear face makes such a decision,
that donkey look-alike, that herder of cows,

that old and decrepit wolf, Ziyâ' the swindler,
whose cheating goads the sheep to kill the shepherd.

That witless buffoon who, when he wants to be kind
and generous, instantly turns Summer into Winter.

If his hand entered the source of the sun,
it would stain its light with the black of night.

If he ever tells something as straight as an arrow,
that thing is also as painfully piercing as the arrow.

When he worships you outwardly, then fear him,
because in his soul he surely wants to hurt you.

He is the sum of lies, hypocrisy, pride and greed.
What gains people have made with that demon!

He is capable of suddenly stopping motes rising to the sky,
if he only thinks of sowing discord between them and the sun.

Anyone standing close to that malevolent man
will lose even the company of his own shadow.

The twin stars near the Great Bear will instantly split up,
if he stands together with them just for a brief instant.

Anyone offering him hospitality, be it for only one night,
will ruin his relationship with his own wife and children.

He creates quarrels between the sword and its sharpness,
every time he spitefully whets the blade of his tongue.[300]

He needs only to gaze absent-mindedly at his hands,
and the nails will grow out and rip his fingers' flesh.

He is so rich that, if he constructed a ladder
from his own coins, it would reach the sky.

In his house he conceals a keg full of gold,
but grudges his servant a mouthful of food.

His wretched wife is too terrified to touch bread,
for fear her husband will denounce her for adultery.

He claims that public devotion is hypocrisy,
and that's why he won't give alms to beggars.

When he gets the chance to indulge in backbiting,
he'll gossip at length about both old and young.

Every simple-hearted person who has placed his trust in him
has met with the same fate as a peasant with a highwayman.

At home his wife is a weaver,
who weaves beautiful cloth:

she makes a mat with hairs from his beard
as a saddle rug for champions' horses.

He claims: 'The science of religious disquisition is my art',
but everything he expounds is the opposite of that science.

His writing is filthier than his beard and whatever he says
is worse than how he says it; yet he criticizes learned imams.

When he claims to give a scientific explanation,
in trying to educate another donkey of his ilk,

sticky words issue from his stammering tongue
just like pieces of shit dripping from a sewer.

In fact I like really shitting right into his mouth,
especially when he claims lineage and a noble house.

Hey brazen face, aren't you ashamed someone like you
asserts he is wiser than all the erudite men of Isfahan?

The only thing you leave in peace and never touch
is your bread, while everybody flees from you.

Hey vile miser, why bother someone like me?
Only he who wants to be damned will do so.

Annoying poets brings no benefits at all,
stupidity can only make people cuckolds.

There can be no doubt that, if the foolish guarded against
the company of the depraved, it would be a good thing.

One day sneering like a goat and playing the cunning fox
will certainly make you a fine morsel for an enraged lion.

You stole two hundredweight of barley from me,
but watch out, this *hejâ* is worth two loads of saffron.

You'll lose that barley when it's eaten by another donkey,
but my lines of poetry will stick on your back for ever.

You would do well to leave alone sharp-tongued people,
who can write *hajv* piercing the chest like javelin tips.

You already fill your belly with other people's bread,
why do you want also to be blamed for other things?

Someone who has depicted a fart as I have
is surely capable of describing a shit like you.

Let anyone who reads these lines, from now to Resurrection Day,
consider it his duty to overwhelm your soul with heaps of curses!

Beware of the people who live in the town of Mazdaqân!
They always try to rob their friends of their possessions!

May every crook who is native of Mazdaqân
be puny, petty and miserable in his homeland![301] *Kamâl od-Din*

The decontextualisation of the satires becomes extreme when not even the name of the *mahju* is mentioned. In such cases there may have been alternative clues to help the contemporary audience identify the person mocked. In the following case, for example, the poet mentions the Lârijân mountains, in northern Iran, as the new home that the 'sordid individual' in question has moved to:

You have got two great whiskers but you are as cowardly as a camel,
you are a donkey-born cow, your arse is a trunk, your balls two flasks.

You are not only wretched but also stingy,
you almost die whenever you glimpse a loaf.

If you simply eat even a morsel of it, O impure beast,
your soul becomes like a dog's out of regret and pain!

When you were young, being fucked was the sole relief for your arse,
it was the only way you could get that beneficial brown ointment.[302]

Now, thanks to your arse, you have everything for the perfect scribe:
its hole is the inkwell, its hairs the ink-soaked cotton in that inkwell.

Your armpits are like a cesspool and your arse is like a sewer,
because of their stench, the spring of your sight has been muddied.

In your eyes, all that is left of humanity is the name,
but it too will soon leave because of that ugly spectacle.

To avoid the shame of seeing your own face
you have become blinder than a bat by day.

But if you want to be able to recover your sight,
eat the cock's soup! Up the arse it's a good broth!

Hey you, shit-eater and husband of a whore,
vile cuckold, dull braggart and lifeless buffoon!

You are a great warrior and, out of fear of you,
an army of fleas will scatter to the right and left.

You found a good home in the Lârijân mountains,
but here you collapse in the abyss left by your arse.

In the hope of radishes pouring in yogurt,
you filled your buttocks' bowl with herbs.[303]

And just how many cocks, in the meantime, have unfastened
the red satin of their hats at the busy loom of your wife's cunt![304]

Qomri

In some cases all references to the identity of the *mahju*, whether proper names or other clues, are omitted:

Because of my tongue you are glum and terrified,
where are all your bold claims and crap now?

Your arse receives all its beauty and honour from a cock,
like a garden become lush thanks to a cypress and a pine.[305] *Labibi*

You are cuckolded by your wife and your sister,
it's no secret, even if no one has spelled it out yet.

How much longer will you insist that your sister is chaste?
It would be better if you kept quiet and didn't say such words!

The only chaste thing in your house is bread,
neither the men nor the women can touch it.[306] *Anvari*

If your mother's skirt had been tied,
as tight as the strings of your food-cloth,

that whore would never have given birth to a cuckold like you,
and the world would have been spared the calamity you are.[307]
Jamâl od-Din

Behaviour and Customs

At times the anonymous *mahju* is even vaguer than in the last poems. The outcome is a sort of proverbial maxim against, for instance, arrogance or faith in reason, as found in the first and second, respectively, of the following examples:

Each owl that wants to fly off with hawks and cranes
will end up with its wings broken and its arse in shreds.[308] *ʿAsjadi*

People who strain their minds
are attempting to milk an ox.

The dress of the stupid suits those persons:
here, with the intellect, you buy only weeds.[309] *ʿOmar Khayyâm*

The general, sententious criticism of certain attitudes may include advice and warnings:

Those limp individuals look like impotent cocks,
when they speak they make only pointless claims.

You should choose men who, through wisdom,
are able to fill your soul with ideas and concepts.[310] *Homâm*

When a son of a noble is impoverished, stay with him!
A branch stripped of flowers will soon be covered in fruit.

But if the son of a poor man becomes rich, avoid him!
The cesspool, when it fills up, stinks worse than before.[311] *Ebn-e Yamin*

The company of an ignorant man is like leather clothing:
it is cumbersome and does not even keep the body warm.

What is even worse than the company of an ignorant man
is that of a relative become important and showing no modesty.

Worse than both is a king who sheds blood
in his own kingdom, and is without mercy.

Lastly, I'll tell you what is worse than all three:
an old man who acts like a youth and isn't ashamed.[312] *Ebn-e Yamin*

The attempt to ignore the passing years, described in the last hemistich, is a frequent topos. Poets usually describe its sexual implications, either directly or in more gentle ways, as in the next two extracts:

Let's suppose that you trick your way into spending the night
with someone, and you make your milk-white hair as black as tar.

When you're with your friend and close the alcove door,
what type of remedy will you find for your dead cock?[313]
Sharaf od-Din Yahyâ al-ʿOwfi

I heard of an elderly man who, recently,
thought of taking a wife in his old age.

He chose a young and beautiful girl called Pearl,
and hid her, like a jewel box, from the eyes of all.

There then ensued the typical scene of a marriage,
but, at the first assault, the old man couldn't get it up.

He drew the bow but was unable to hit the target:
a thick cloth can only be sown with a steel needle.

He began to complain to his friends and look for excuses,
saying that the impertinent girl had emptied his house.

Rows and quarrels broke out between the husband and wife,
and this reached the police chief and came before the judge.

'All of these problems and these contrasts are not the girl's fault'
I said to him 'if your hand trembles, how can you thread a pearl?'[314]

Sa'di

Moral teachings about behaviour and customs may be obviously found in mystical poems. The following example highlights the pointlessness of earthly striving and pomposity:

A king had a castle built with gold ornaments,
which had cost hundreds of thousands of dinars.

When this heavenly castle was complete,
he had it furnished with carpets and hangings,

and people who came from every part
brought precious offerings in homage.

The king summoned his wise men and companions,
and beckoned them to sit on benches beside him.

He asked: 'What does my castle
lack in beauty and perfection?'

They replied: 'In all the world, no one
has ever seen nor will see anything like it!'

But an ascetic there got to his feet and declared to the king:
'O you of noble fortune, a crack has been left, a terrible flaw.

If your beautiful castle was complete without this crack,
the castle of paradise itself would pay homage from heaven.'

The king replied: 'I've seen no crack in my castle,
O ignorant man! Do you want to stir up trouble?'

The ascetic continued: 'O you, who are distinguished by royalty,
the crack is the one which will be opened by the angel of death.

Let's hope that you will fill it in properly, otherwise
what will you do with your castle, crown and throne?

Although this castle is as joyous as paradise,
death will make it appear ugly in your eyes.

Nothing lasts for ever: our existence
is transient. What remedy to this?

Don't brag about your dwelling and castle,
don't goad the horse of pride and haughtiness!

If someone then discovers a flaw
in your noble condition, woe to you!'[315] *'Attâr*

Even in mystical poems, as mentioned in the introduction, the authors have no scruples about resorting to bawdy language in order to express their moral beliefs and capture and persuade the audience. The following story is a classic example of this. In an inextricable blend of humour and seriousness, the poet obscenely describes and condemns concupiscence, which blinds the ability to learn, and greed, which prevents any distinction between the forms and substance of life:

A maid was in the habit of pulling a donkey onto herself,
because she was so very lecherous and greatly depraved.

She had accustomed that animal to coitus,
teaching it how human beings couple.

The cunning girl always made use of a gourd,
which she fitted on the donkey's cock as a stop.

That wretched girl wore it to ensure that,
when they coupled, only half the cock got in.

If the whole cock had penetrated her,
it would have ripped her womb and guts.

But after a while the donkey gradually began to waste away,
and the lady of the house was puzzled seeing it as thin as a hair.

She took the animal to the farrier to enquire of him
what disease could have reduced it to such a state.

The donkey seemed quite healthy,
and the secret wasn't discovered.

The lady decided to investigate further,
and devoted all her time to the problem.

It's right that the soul should take its commitments seriously,
anyone who seeks seriously will eventually find an answer.

She thus began to pay close attention to the donkey's affairs,
and found that the little narcissus of her maid lay beneath it.

Spying the scene through a crack in the door,
she came in for an even bigger surprise:

the donkey began to penetrate the servant
in the same way men penetrate women.

She was struck by envy and said: 'If this is possible,
I should get precedence since the donkey belongs to me.'

The donkey had been instructed and trained,
the table was ready and the lamp was lit.

She pretended to have seen nothing and knocked on the door,
saying: 'Have you much more sweeping to do in the house?'

And to confuse things further, she continued:
'O my young girl, I'm here, open the door!'

Then she went silent and said nothing more to the girl,
concealing the secret for the purposes of her own pleasure.

The maid put away all her illicit things,
and, stepping forward, went to the door.

She made her face look pained with moist eyes,
and rubbed her lips as if to say: 'I'm fasting.'

She also picked up and brandished a soft brush,
to make it seem she'd been sweeping the room.

When, with the broom in hand, she appeared at the door,
the lady murmured to herself: 'O you cunning vixen,

you pulled a pained face and picked up the broom,
but why is the donkey so far from its pasture?

It has been caught in the middle of the act, and is now angrily
waiting for you, eyes on the door and cock swinging about.'

She said this to herself, without revealing anything to the girl,
whom she treated courteously as if nothing had happened.

Then she told her: 'Put on your chador,
go to that house, take a message from me,

say these things, and do these other tasks!'
This, in short, was the meeting they had,

and it is enough for now to convey the essence of the story.
Once the maid had been sent away, that wary old woman,

elated with the drunkenness of lust,
closed the door behind her and said:

'Now I'm alone and can shout
my joy: I am rid of all hindrances!'

The woman was so enthusiastic that she grew more lecherous,
excited as she was by the great fire of her lust for that donkey.

But those carnal instincts deceived her,
as happens when a fool is caught out.

Lustfulness makes the heart of people blind and deaf,
so a donkey may look like Joseph and a fire like a light.[316]

O how many drunk with fire or in search of it
believe themselves to be the absolute light.

Only the help of a servant of God or the calling to God
can put them back on the right path and change their attitude,

making them see that the image of fire
is only a false thing on their long way.

Greediness makes ugly things seem very beautiful,
and lust is the worst disaster besetting the right path:

it has shamed a hundred thousand good names,
it has confused a hundred thousand wise men.

If lust has given a donkey the looks of Joseph of Egypt,
what looks, then, will that Judean lust give Joseph?

If its enchantment makes dung look like honey,
what will it make honey like at a time of temptation?

Lust comes from eating: cut down on your food
or get married, and you'll be able to flee from evil.

If you overeat, it drives you to illicit things,
what goes in must find some way out!

Marriage, in this case, is a divine formula,
so that the devil won't cast you into misfortune.

If you are greedy for food, find a wife at once,
or else the cat will come and steal your provisions.

Immediately bring to a halt the kicking donkey
with a load of stones, before it can dominate you.

If you don't know the effect of fire, avoid it!
Don't hang around it, if you are inexperienced.

You must learn the art of pots and stoves,
or you will burn the soup and the pan.

You need water and you must be skilful,
if you want everything to be cooked right.

If you don't know the art of the blacksmith,
you'll burn your beard and hair in his smithy.

The woman closed the door, joyfully pulled the donkey
towards her, and inevitably received her just reward.

She dragged it into the middle of the room,
and then lay down under it on her back.

Resting on the bench where she'd seen her maid,
she hoped, that whore, to satisfy her own desire.

She raised her legs and when the donkey stuck it in,
that cock lit up a huge fire and it blazed within her.

The well-trained donkey pressed it into the woman
up to its balls, and the woman perished on the spot.

The strokes of that cock had burst her liver,
while all her guts had been torn to shreds.

She had no time even to sigh before yielding her soul,
and she fell to one side while the bench fell to the other.

The room filled with blood and the woman hung head down.
She died instantly: 'Fate's uncertainty' robbed her of her soul.[317]

O father, what an evil death with great ignominy.
Have you ever seen a martyr of a donkey's cock?

Listen to what is the 'chastisement of humiliation'[318]
in the Koran: don't sacrifice your life in such disgrace!

You should know that concupiscence is like a jackass,
being under it is more vile than that jackass itself.

If you die of selfishness on the road of concupiscence,
then you can be certain you are similar to that woman.

God gives our concupiscence the aspect of the donkey
because He creates forms according to their nature.

This is the secret that will be revealed on Resurrection Day,
for God's sake, eschew your body, which is like a donkey!

The Lord warned the infidels with fire,
but they said: 'Better fire than shame!'

He replied: 'But the source of all shame is a fire,
it's the same fire that destroyed this woman!'

In her greed she craved for an enormous mouthful,
but it stuck in her throat and presaged a brutal death.

O greedy one, eat with moderation
even the most delicate sweetmeats.

God, may He be praised, has in this way given voice
to the balance. Read the Sura of The All-merciful![319]

Be careful not to lose your balance through too much longing,
cupidity and greed are enemies leading you to perdition.

He who is greedy wants everything and so loses everything,
don't be a slave to greed, O turnip-head and son of a turnip-head!

As the maid was leaving the house, she said to herself:
'Alas, my lady, you have chosen to send the expert away!

You'll try to do things without a master,
and so you will foolishly lose your life.

You have stolen an incomplete lesson from me,
and were ashamed to ask if there was a trick!'

If a bird pecks the grain from the ear of wheat,
it will not be in danger of falling into a trap.

Eat with great discretion and don't go stuffing yourself full.
First recite: 'Eat and drink!' and then: 'but be you not prodigal!'[320]

In this way you can have your food without any danger,
thanks to wisdom and to contentment, and so be it!

The wise man gathers good fortune, not pain, from the world,
while the ignoramus has nothing other than many regrets:

as soon as the rope tightens round his neck,
he'll no longer be able to swallow his food.

Can a bird savour the grain in a trap?
Eating it in a trap is like taking poison.

Only thoughtless birds would eat grain found there,
just as ordinary people fall into the trap of this world.

Conscientious and shrewd birds
are careful to avoid that grain.

The grain in a trap is mortal food,
any bird seeking that grain is blind.

The Lord of the trap will cut off the head of the stupid,
but He brings the thoughtful to His own gatherings:

for the former, only the body counts,
while the latter can sing in every key.

The maid returned and, through the crack in the door,
saw her lady lying dead, there beneath the donkey.

She said: 'O stupid woman, could this have happened
if the master had shown you how it should be done?

You only saw the exterior, the secret was concealed from you,
you didn't learn anything but still persevered in that business!

To you that cock seemed like honey and a date cake.
O greedy woman, why didn't you notice the gourd?

Blinded by your passion for that donkey,
the gourd remained hidden from your gaze.

You only superficially paid attention to your master,
and thought, quite satisfied, you had learnt the art.'

There are many stupid and ignorant hypocrites,
who, faced with holy men, only note their cowl.

And many brazen-faced ones who, through inexperience,
learn from the great to talk and brag only about themselves:

one, holding his club in hand, saying: 'I am Moses',
another, breathing on the stupid, claiming: 'I am Jesus!'

Alas, when the time of the test comes,
you're asked for the sincerity of the sincere!

Go and ask the master for the rest of the subject!
Or, as well as being greedy, are you blind and deaf?

If you try to have everything, you will lose everything,
and you will be one of that bunch of idiots prey to wolves!

You should not only pay attention to the form of words
repeating them like a parrot: you must grasp their meaning![321] *Rumi*

At times the criticism of immorality within satires seems to be aimed not so much at people but at institutions and customs themselves. Thus, for example, we have the following curious and bold mocking of arranged marriages:

> Once upon a time in the north,
> there was a greedy rich man.
>
> He had an ugly, bad-tempered daughter
> who loved clothes above everything else.
>
> But clearly damask and brocade
> cannot suit girls with no beauty.
>
> Her father gave her as a bride to a handsome man with silver limbs,
> and, at the ceremony, asked him for a huge sum as a guarantee.[322]
>
> Eager to enjoy her first night of marriage in the best way,
> the maiden daubed her body with the sweetest scents.
>
> It was like coating counterfeit coins with silver,
> or mixing amber perfume with armpit stink.
>
> When she swiftly removed from her ugly face
> the gold-embroidered veil she was wearing,
>
> her husband immediately realised his terrible luck
> and cruel fate: hell's door opened to this heavenly man!
>
> All night he held his face turned to the wall,
> because he didn't want to behold that spectacle.
>
> Several times his new bride badgered him,
> pulling his clothes in order to be embraced.
>
> That young man became totally dismayed
> by such misfortune. Forcing a smile, he said:
>
> 'You'd make even a minaret limp,
> and you want desire to grow in me?
>
> You're a greater affliction than the angel of death!
> I'd rather be stung by a scorpion than touched by you!'

He droswsed until dawn, meditating on his fate,
he was desperate, beating one hand on the other.

In the end he realised he couldn't put up a fight,
and he also saw that the way out was closed.

He thought for a long time on what he could do,
he certainly didn't want to waste his life like this.

Meanwhile, sorrow had reached the depths of his heart,
that thought was like a spine pricking him to the bone.

He decided to tell his father-in-law the way things stood:
'O you, who know what justice is and are inclined to good,

until now you have treated me kindly,
you have been so courteous and generous

that even long years would not be enough
for me to thank you for your favours.

So, if you can, order that my feet
be freed from the snare of this sorrow!

A husband and a wife marry each other
thinking only to live in love and agreement,

but I have no peace and she is unhappy:
find a remedy for our miserable condition!'

Raising his head, the old man replied:
'Don't keep harping on about it, my friend!

Either you adapt to the pains and pleasures of the world,
or you'll end up in prison. Can you pay for a divorce?'

Hearing such unpleasant words spoken by the old man,
the young man was stunned and didn't know what to say.

He asked for help from the elders of the place,
and called on a myriad of people to intercede.

The old man paid no heed to any of them,
nothing he listened to would move him.

The young man felt desperate and nailed by misfortune,
the sea of his great worries seemed to have no shores.

So, neglecting his wife, he began
to court her sister and won her heart.

And one night, slipping into her bed,
he put his stick into her ivory phial.

Given her tender age, the girl began to scream,
but he closed her mouth with a fistful of gold.

He laid her face to the ground with her buttocks in the air,
and stuck it up her behind, easily pushing up to his balls.

He thus placed his cheek to her cheek, his hands
on her neck, navel on navel and pestle in the mortar.

After this he decided to try his brother-in-law,
and take down the breeches of his honour.

He found the house empty and saw a thick tail,
his cat leapt up and ripped the tablecloth.

He also gave his mother-in-law her due,
setting her down with her legs in the air.

Then he decided that it was the turn of his wife's aunts:
the paternal one had syrup, the maternal one a bougie.

Next, he decided to console his wife's nurse,
and beguiled her with kindness and sweet words.

He inquired where she slept and lived,
and finally found the street and house.

One festive evening he went there with his candle,
and promptly stuck half of it up between her thighs.

He also pursued and then fucked
a young girl employed by his wife.

He gently set her down on her knees,
and did everything in the proper way.

The slender girl didn't like this business,
and began to kick out and twist about.

In the end, however, he tamed her like a colt,
and stuck his cock up her crystalline arse.

He went all the way, and unspeakable things happened.
He couldn't have threaded a lovelier pearl than that!

Then, he took care of his wife's maid,
and, making every effort to do his best,

filled her jar with a portion of yogurt,
so that she wouldn't envy the others.

And anyone else he met in that family,
he had them from the front or rear.

He wielded his steel horn on those people,
like a sword reaping death all around.

The neighbours knew everything that was happening,
yet couldn't do anything to stop such indecencies.

But a roll of drums can't be concealed,
and so an endless scandal was born.

Acquaintances and friends of the bride's father
went to tell the old man what was going on.

It was a blow for that poor fellow,
he closed his shop and hurried away.

He picked up the bag with the marriage contract,
and rushed to take it to his lustful son-in-law.

'I don't want any money, if you ask for a divorce', he said,
'I'll leave you the dowry, the clothes and land, but go away!'

On hearing these words from the old man,
the helpless groom was amazed and speechless.

Tears began to flow from his eyes,
on realising he could finally be happy.

And he said: 'O my lord and patron,
what have I done to receive this order?'

The other replied: 'Don't say anything!
This house is too small for the two of us!

Of all the people who live with us here,
I'm the only poor wretch to have been spared.

All the others, whether they be male or female,
you good-for-nothing, you have raped them all.

If one night you decided to jump on me,
O lewd demon, who would come to my aid?'

'I'd never commit this crime', replied the other,
'and I don't want to leave my sweet bride!'

The old man's companions and friends
jumped on the young man from all sides.

He began a fight with each of them, and the brawl
only ceased when the divorce was agreed upon.

That victim, who no longer even dreamed of being saved,
at long last managed to free himself from the mortal snare.

His cheeks began to bloom again,
and strutting about he murmured:

'It's not wise to suffer and sigh,
force can only be met with force!'

Take care to avoid bad company, and may God
'guard us against the chastisement of the fire!'[323] *Saʿdi*

The next poem is critical of the very idea of marriage and the family routine, whose boredom and strain are blamed on the woman:

A son implored his father saying:
'Please, help me find a good wife!'

'My dear son, fornicate if you wish', he responded,
'but don't take a wife! Learn from others, not from me!

If you commit adultery and then a guard arrests you,
he'll let you go for he's already caught so many like you.

But if you go and take a wife, she'll never let you make off!
And if you leave her, you've no idea what trouble she'll stir up.

Why do you want to follow in the footsteps of your mother and me?
You've seen these situations, and I have seen even more of them!

Avoid the naggings about bread and firewood!
Look at your dad's beard, less than half is left!'[324] *Owhadi*

Another aspect of household life dealt with is the relationship between the lord and his slaves. The following poem describes the advantageous purchase of a poor slave, and his rapid and unexpected transformation:

At the bazaar I bought a young Indian slave,
for so little, I'm ashamed even to mention it.

As wretched as an arse, fragile as a cunt,
stinking like pitch and as black as ink,

he had a grim sour face, teeth like a pomegranate slice,
and instead of balls he had two lumps of rotten meat.

He had suffered so much he was as lifeless and as puny as an ant,
he was so weak he slithered about like a snake, with no hands or feet.

Covered in nits, his head was like a piece of silk with poppy seeds,
and his armpits stank as much as a burnt carcass within a grave.

Round his mouth was so dried up, it was encrusted with salt,
and his cheeks were so rough that they looked like a broom.

He was bent on his knees because of his unhappy state,
and his eyes were sunk into their sockets through hunger.

With big balls and a tiny face, he really looked like a monkey,
but his long nails and short hair made him more like a hyena.

He was like a seed without a root, a root without a trunk,
a trunk without a branch and a branch without fruit.

I took him home, anointed his head, combed his hair,
and bought him a hat and a garment with a pair of trousers.

In a couple of months he was totally transformed,
and began to do a little of all the domestic chores.

He was a groom, a valet sorting clothes, a steward,
a butler and a book-keeper for income and expenses.

If he heard me fart, he said: 'God bless you',
if he saw a fly on me, he chased it off like a snake.

He became so kind, scrupulous and prompt
that I believed it right to treat him affectionately.

I thus took to looking after him with every care,
and he grew graceful, deserving kisses and embraces.

He became a heavenly flower, to the awe of the celestial creatures,
he became an idol worthy of a temple, envied by all the other idols:

refined, wise, polite and charming,
gentle, dashing, elegant and obliging.

He learned to drink wine, sing melodies, recount amusing things,
use very eloquent phrases and confidently expound concepts.

His ways became so imbued with sweetness
that I amusingly dubbed him Black Sugar.

I felt a strong desire to fuck him: whatever could be more appropriate!
He was sweeter than the best sugar, and handsomer than a painting!

One night, I lay down and said: 'Caress the feet of your lord,
because his wild heart is suffering greatly on your account!'

So he embraced my feet, and with his hand
caressed them as tenderly as only the Sufis do.

Like the worst of sinners I pulled him under me,
adopting the credo that any prohibition is misbelief.

I fucked him with the kindness of a Zoroastrian Magus
when he fucks his sister, but with even more love.[325]

When I fell asleep, he got up and, to get his own back,
slipped his cucumber in my hole and stuck it up.

In the middle of the night I woke and noticed that
my slave's cucumber was hooked on my flask.

It was like a nightmare: he had put me under in such a way
that I could hardly breathe and thought I was on death's door.

I screamed and said: 'What are you doing? I'm not a girl!
Stop fucking me, you've made me all sore and worn!'

Because of my rough manner he grew angry and exclaimed:
'What! Were you dead when I fucked you a hundred times?

But no sooner were you sated than you woke up, you brazen face!
These refusals are certainly not very nice after such a warm welcome!'

I have poured out my heart, and now I end
this story to put a halt to all these trifles.

With a thousand strategies and tricks,
I'd turned my servant into a feeble pansy.

But then, from under my cock, he jumped up like a true bugger.
This is a lesson you should learn, O you, who are so sharp of sight![326]

Mokhtâri

Sometimes the poet's irony goes beyond the household setting to focus on more social and public traditions such as oracles and omens:

If your right ball starts quivering,
you'll have wealth and no trouble.

If, on the contrary, it's your left ball that quivers,
you'll have a son and welcome that little darling.

Finally, if both balls quiver at the same time,
you'll be a king and enjoy great satisfaction.[327] *Badr-e Jâjarmi*

If your arse suddenly quivers,
you'll have news of good luck.

If your right buttock quivers,
your enemy will slander you.

If your left buttock quivers,
you'll get rich and be happy.[328] *Badr-e Jâjarmi*

CHAPTER 3

Burlesque Poetry

Form and Content

Burlesque poetry is wide-ranging and embraces different kinds of humorous re-workings of serious poetry, in terms of form and/or content. We have already encountered features of this type in some of the compositions quoted above. Among the famous examples is a satirical version of the clashes—as narrated by Ferdowsi in the *Shâhnâme*—between the Persian army (here represented by the legendary Rostam),[329] and the troops of the Turanian sovereign Afrâsiyâb (Humân and Pirân, mentioned in the following lines, are commanders of these troops). In this approach the imagery and vocabulary of the classical epic are mixed with desecrating elements, while the rhyming-couplet structure and metrical pattern of the model are preserved:

The great Rostam, that valiant hero,
undid his breeches and knelt down.

Humân raised his prick, as fast as smoke,
doing just as Pirân had ordered him to,

and he slipped it up the split in Rostam's arse,
which, sorely wounded, soon began to burn.

Then it was Humân's turn to go beneath,
and Rostam, like a courageous lion,

stuck such a hard cock up him
that Humân's arse was wrecked.

Those two swordsmen had wrecked arses,
but became two of the most celebrated heroes.

O brother, if you want to be a champion,
you should listen carefully to my words:

'Lie down with your arse upwards,
and show off your qualities clearly.

Anyone who is passing by will be able to screw you,
and you, thanks to those cocks up you, will be gratified!'

No one can remain in this world for ever,
it's good that a fine memory of us lives on.[330] *'Obeyd*

In addition to the epic, other poetic genres are also borrowed for burlesque poetry, as in the following examples. The first is related to the lyric and the author parodies the classical descriptions of Spring in the 10th-century Khorasanian-style exordia of *qaside*, crossing over the typical lexicon and imagery of 'Onsori and Farrokhi with obscene and grotesque expressions:[331]

Spring's army has again launched a surprise attack,
furiously tearing out each of Winter's whiskers.

Warmth's hand has pulled the beard of cold,
just as Moses pulled the beard of Aaron.[332]

December filled the world with flour,
a cloud up in the sky was its mill.

Now the Spring breeze has stolen
all that white wealth from the earth.

The cloud opens up its trousers and pisses
on the mountains, valleys, plains and deserts.

Thanks to those heavy showers, in the wide expanses
rivers like the Amu Darya and the Syr Darya start to flow.

Because of the wind, the water of the pond
is like a decrepit old man's pock-marked face.

Thunder rumbles overhead: you would think
someone is wrecking the arse of a boy with no pay.

The whole earth has been adorned, just as the state
is adorned, thanks to the justice of the prince Fâzlun.[333]

O God, may the abundant table of his good fortune
never be bare, from the Tigris to the Amu Darya![334] *Dibâji*

In the next example, the parodic structure is more elaborate and concerns the various components of a *qaside*, mocked in both the lyrical and panegyrical sections. This time the first part outrageously imitates (through allusions and not merely direct licentiousness) the amorous variant of the exordium of the corresponding serious poetry (here the beloved is the male member), and ends with a clever transitional section based on an obscene idea introducing the panegyric. The panegyric is organised in a traditional style for some lines before ending with a finale in *hazl* tones:

O comfort of the heart of Khosrow, desire of the heart of Shirin,[335]
beautiful sweet red-headed creature, you bow your head but are bold,

you have a belt round your waist like that of Khosrow,
and the crown on your head is similar to that of Shirin.[336]

Farhâd would have had Shirin sooner or later,
if he had had a club with all your strength.

Your crown remained concealed until you tied the belt,
you put it round your waist, and the crown appeared.

To celebrate that crown and that belt,
the populace embellished the whole city.

You are the king of limbs, and crown and belt suit you well.
It is only natural! All kings have both a crown and a belt!

You don't have any eyes, no, and not even any feet,
but you move confidently and find your way with ease.

With friends and strangers, O courageous hero,
you can sit up or lie on the top of a regal seat.

Whenever you want to sit, you can do so on a throne,
whenever you want to lie, a cushion is always ready.[337]

But you seem to feel rancour in your heart and soul,
even though you are the object of so much love:

you want to get the beloved of heart and soul down,
and you spitefully mete out your revenge on his arse.

You gently begin to embrace him and then violently
push in up to your balls: woe to him who lingers there!

When you swell up with air, you will burn like fire. If you don't pour
your water fast, the wretch beneath you will end up under the ground.

Get up whoever you want, as long as you are far from my arse,
O you, who are as deranged as the devil and twisted like a dragon.

This is the interpretation that Ebn-e Sirin gives[338]
to anyone who has seen your image in a dream:

'If you take even only one half of it while awake,
your horse's harness will be full of rubies and gems.'

The destiny of your arse is really like that of a wall
or an anvil, since everything depends on how it is struck.

Hey you, who go round offering your arse to all!
Stop for a moment, so I can tell you who to take it to:

give it to that prince who relieves sufferers,
and has a cock which makes poor people rich.

His cock is even better than the one I've so sincerely described:
what I have in mind is the unmatchable cock of Safi od-Din,

the wise Asir ol-Molk, that noble and generous prince,
who receives compliments from the heavenly vault,

that *qibla* of good fortune, thanks to whose greatness
the kingdom of the East and China is happy and prosperous.

He pours more coins on the head of beggars
than the drops that rain on flowers in Spring.

To be sure: when his munificent hand dispenses gold all around him,
the unlucky and poor get as rich and generous as Hâtem and Afshin.[339]

When a destitute pilgrim goes to visit him,
he comes away from that court full of goods.[340]

On the chessboard of power he is stronger than the castle,
for the munificent king he is worth more than the queen.

These are serious matters, but now I'll go back to witty things,
thank God whatever I say shines like the moon and the Pleiades,

and at your court, O generous prince, all my lines of verse,
both serious and facetious, are prized more than I expected.

Whosoever, then, derides fortune in your court,
sort him out with that whip of yours, full of *dugh*![341]

Whoever feels bitterness towards you, even as little as a sesame seed,
empty him for good of all filthy sediment with your strong arrow.[342]

If anyone envies you and, in anguish, tears out his own beard,
drop a heap of shit on that beard each day and month of the year!

With the Chinese idols make your feast as happy as a temple,
and fill it with tulips, narcissuses, lilies and wild roses.

Arrange the curls of those idols so they are nicely braided,
and crush the arse of your enemy's wife like a smooth cunt.

Power is like a woman who needs good fortune as a husband,
and for that woman's cunt there's nothing better than your cock.

Only your good fortune is worthy of such a cunt and such a woman,
while I wish castration and impotence for anyone envying you.

May good fortune bid farewell to that enemy who is so full of envy,
and leave him gloomy, his cock limp on his balls and the dowry to pay.[343]

Suzani

Another variant of the classical exordium of *qaside* is provided by *chistân* (riddles). There are licentious adaptations of this variant, as in the following riddle with its obvious solution:

Who is that dear creature with a crown of rubies
on its head and who always wears a pink silk cloak?

A red being, swollen with arrogance, pin-eyed and hard-hearted,
his usual resting place is the black clothes of the Abbasid dynasty.[344]

He's limp like a sick man but, when he wants to,
he leaps up like a thief escaping from his chains.

He has merely managed to learn the street sweeper's trade,
it's strange that at times he's covered with silver or with gold.[345]

Like any sword sullied with blood he is well sharpened,
and properly sheathed up the behind of moon-cheeked boys.

He sheds the innocent children's blood on the ground,
and then, from his single eye, pours out clear tears.

He breathes down the necks of harmless creatures and eats their shit:
who knows what his reward will be in the end for such bad deeds!

When he's hard, even the devil tries to escape his blows,
since he'll jump out at you from nowhere like a shooting star.

His stature is equal to that of an arrow,
with a carnelian tip and musk feathers.[346]

He's like a needle made of ruby,
but cuts through like sharp shears.

When he stands up straight, he's like a red-gemmed candle,
set on a black candlestick made of ambergris and musk.

He's as precise as a book-keeper but strangely in his accounts
ninety and twenty are the only numbers that ever come out.[347]

If he stays as a guest in a friend's house even only for a while,
he deliberately vomits on all the doors and on all the walls.

When the time of an attack comes, his head swells up with pride,
and that's why they lop it off, just as they do to the king's enemies.[348]

Ebn-e Yamin

Continuing our survey of burlesque poetry, in the following *tarji'band* the author emulates the protest typical of many *rendi* poems, i.e. poems describing the attitude and the deeds of the debauchees, in which heretical symbols are exalted as a sign of contempt for social norms and conventions. With mocking and obscene tones, in this case the poet takes the defiance of these compositions to extremes: the effect seems to be the quintessence of *rendi* verse, so impregnated with its spirit that it becomes not only a sign of contempt for the orthodoxy of official doctrines but also a critique and ironic supersession of the traditional and excessively 'moderate' *rendi* verse itself.

The time has come to set to work,
and to make our heretical habits clear.

Let's go and dwell in the quarter of the Magi,[349]
and turn our gaze towards the Tartar *qibla*.

If this age doesn't give us a hand,
let's stick it up the arse of the age!

How much longer do we want to suffer for an arse?
How much longer do we want to wait for a cunt?

If we can't get to the arse and the cunt,
best leave them and choose a good wank!

Come on then, take a seat, my dear friend!
As long as you can, there is nothing better:

> have a wank, for wanking is pleasurable,
> and all the more pleasurable under the cowl!

Without money things don't end well,
on the way of love you need plenty cash.

Boys only yield when they are paid,
and whores never with anyone for free.

Happily squander, therefore, all your goods,
before destiny steals them in one fell swoop.

Sit down for an instant, with a pure soul,
beside generous people, so you have peace,

and suffer less in pursuing the charms of the arse and the cunt,
because they will never solve any of your problems for you.

Unlike those cuckolds who seek the arse,
unlike those puny men who screw the cunt,

> have a wank, for wanking is pleasurable,
> and all the more pleasurable under the cowl!

O friends, the cock's affairs are no joke,
no one has ever seen such long things.

When the cock rises up like a flag,
it's as splendid as champion's banner.

It's fine for fucking like a donkey and for wanking off,
but anything else it's capable of is nothing but illusion.

There's nothing better than witty words,
when speaking of amorous relations:

it's best your cock prostrates itself before an arse,
since the *mehrâb* of the cunt is not suited to prayer.[350]

You may even give your soul to conquer an arse,
but, if things don't go well for you these days,

> have a wank, because wanking is pleasurable,
> and all the more pleasurable under the cowl.

We are such miserable impostors,
wanton, verbose, dirty scoundrels.

Day and night we are at our beloved's side,
we're constantly in the company of lovers.

We languish in the pursuit of sweet-lipped heartbreakers,
we always die for the sake of a beloved with jasmine legs.

And we oppose in this way cold preachers,
making war on the little hypocrite sheikh.

But now we will give up arses and cunts,
even although, I know, we lust after them.

If you have a little wit, O my dear brother,
listen to our advice, the advice of wankers:

> have a wank, for wanking is pleasurable,
> and all the more pleasurable under the cowl!

Day and night we roam the city
in search of the wine-seller's house.

We are completely drunk on those bold courageous boys,
we are smitten by those moon-faced handsome creatures,

we are prisoners in the snare of their curls,
and are caught in the strings of their eyebrows,

so we feel safe in this vile age,
sheltered from its every evil deed.

But if no cunt or arse comes into our hand,
we, who are hard, callous and dissolute,

will sit down, pull out our cocks,
and, as we merrily wank, we'll sing:

> have a wank, for wanking is pleasurable,
> and all the more pleasurable under the cowl!

How much longer do you want to suffer from the world,
O heart? You must no longer accept our pain and yours!

Ignore the things of the world!
Free yourself from every bond!

Arse and cunt are simply two wrecks,
the first is full of shit, the second of stench.

Leave them both, as befits true men,
who are free of women and boys.

And when your cock gets hard,
listen to me, don't mock yourself!

Sit down, close the door, whet your hand,
and don't stop, do what the lewd Sufis do:

> have a wank, for wanking is pleasurable,
> and all the more pleasurable under the cowl!

As long as you can, spend your time with libertines and drunks,
enjoy yourself with them and drink wine in front of everyone.

Empty your glass to the sound of tambourines and bells,
never spend a moment without the wine of the Magi.

Happy is only the man who, out of drunkenness,
never worries about himself, not even for an instant.

Although these whores and big lads
give their cunts and arses for a trifle,

don't roar any more after a cunt,
no longer hurt your soul for an arse.

Forget about both of them and set yourself free,
and, never ceasing, like libertines and the rabble,

have a wank, for wanking is pleasurable,
and all the more pleasurable under the cowl!

Look only for the Magi's wine from us,
don't tell us anything but love stories!

Only sit down beside beautiful people,
and hang out at the wine-seller's shop!

Don't complain about the violence of fate
and don't expect any loyalty from this age!

Revel, always be happy, smile with joy,
and fart on the beards of spiteful little men!

O you generous breath of zephyr,
be kind and don't invent excuses,

run off and, please, say to the local preacher,
on behalf of 'Obeyd-e Zâkâni, how things are:

have a wank, for wanking is pleasurable,
and all the more pleasurable under the cowl![351] *'Obeyd*

Replies to Poems

Among the most common structures used to convey burlesque poetry are the so-called *javâb*, kinds of 'replies' to poems written by other authors. In this case the replies are usually in the same metre and rhyme as the originals, but are used for differente purposes and in a playful way to provoke surprise and amusement. A circumstantiated understanding of this kind of poetry would obviously require a presentation of the models and their contexts, which for reasons of space is not possible here. At times these replies are a mixture of *tazmin* (quotations) taken from the models and new hemistichs or lines composed for the occasion. Significant works of this type are the following examples by Boshâq and Qâri, who reworked classical ghazals, the former by borrowing culinary terminology and the second by introducing sartorial expressions:[352]

If, as happens in Khorasan, a bowl of that soup is placed before me,
I would give Samarkand and Bukhara for the fragrance of its meat.

If you have yellow rice and almond cake, then hold dear
the banks of Roknâbâd and the flower gardens of Mosallâ.

Whyever enrich the taste of the sorbet with saffron and musk?[353]
Does a beautiful face need make-up and colours, a mole and down?

The goodness of roast lamb and the deliciousness of stewed mutton tail
have stripped patience from the heart, just as the Turks plunder the table.

Don't investigate the mysteries of stuffed tripe and their hidden secrets!
No one has ever solved, or will ever solve, this enigma through thought.

From the fragrance of those sauced giblets cheering up the spirit,
I realised this food would soon divert me from my usual diet.

Tell us about the bunches of exquisite Muscat grapes, O Boshâq,
and the firmament will spread the Pleiades' necklace on your poems.[354]

Boshâq

He who has precious new cloth should give away his old piece,
we wrote down only one point in our notebook, and it is this.

If I put my finger in the buttonhole, as if it were in a ring,
I rule Solomon's hundred realms because of that seal.[355]

The inevitable fate of a ragged cloth and a silk cloak was always
that the first was a bazaar beauty, while the second hid from sight.

A cowl goes with rough skin and the tunic with leather boots,
that is how things stand in the perennial cycle of destiny.

From any person who considers Chinese brocade to be shoddy cloth,
I won't purchase drawings, *even though he were the Painter of China.*[356]

The prayer rug will not divert the heart from its brush,
it's an old situation that will endure until the last day.

O Qâri, tear your old clothes in the hope of new ones,
if you look carefully, your own good lies just in this.[357]

Qâri

For his part, ʿObeyd offers wittily obscene contributions to this kind of reply:

> Once the cock said to the cunt: 'O you, my favourite idol,
> *last night, in the absence of your face, a fire rose to my head.'*
>
> The cunt replied: 'I swear it on your soul! With the arse,
> *we mentioned your name many times all night long.*
>
> *Wherever I turned my eyes, your image*
> *was painted in every corner of the room.*
>
> Until the first light of day, out of desire for your figure,
> *water continually flowed from my eye, dampening the earth.'*[358] *ʿObeyd*

> Last night, smelling the stink of a cunt, my cock exclaimed:
> *'Here's the scent which comes from the Muliyân brook.'*
>
> A wind came out from the buttocks and the cock, standing up, said:
> *'This is the scent of a kind friend, a scent which arrives from afar.'*[359]
> *ʿObeyd*

At other times the reply follows a logic less closely bound to the original poem, and the resulting compositions are basically independent of the content of the model. They are often recognisable as replies because of a declaration by the poet, which, as in the following two cases, is usually placed in the final line. The first is a reply by Suzani to Moʿezzi and has the formal requisites of the genre, since it adopts the same metre, rhyme and refrain as the model.[360] In terms of content it is certainly outrageous:

> Yesterday I ran into an idol in the street,
> and her gait seemed like that of the moon:
>
> she was provocative, sweet as sugar, like a cypress,
> a nimble little whore more beautiful than the sun.
>
> I stopped and tried to stand in her way,
> so the heartbreaker had to walk by me.
>
> I boldly put some questions to her and,
> in truth, she was very forward in her talk.

I asked her to be my guest but she answered that
she'd thought of going elsewhere after leaving home.

I said to her: 'Before fate, the will succumbs,
only what our destiny ordains ever happens!

When one fate is awaiting us,
only the thoughtless seek another.

Let us go to my alcove and spend some time together,
the silver of your chest will change everything to gold.

There you'll find wine, kebab, a backgammon set and a harp,
and, as you know, those four things make people happy!'

She liked my sweet talk and, with my flattering,
her stony heart began to grow a little gentler.

In short, I took that moon home with me,
a moon that was an ornament to every star.

Before I could even place food in front of her, she said:
'Where's the wine, the sovereign of the two worlds?'

She seized a great big cup and gulped it down,
and in that way I saw a moon tasting wine.

Then she set down the backgammon board,
placed the pieces and began her clever moves,

but we made no more than three
and the game abruptly ended.

She eventually took up the harp,
and played a series of melodies:

she sang a ghazal in the style of Nowruz songs,
with a rhythm typical of victories and triumphs.

In my passion for her, my eyes dried up and my heart melted.
I was upset: I wept silver tears and my face yellowed like gold.

She made a kebab of my heart and drew wine from my eyes,
even though she had real provisions ready alongside her.

I begged her to be good and kind that night,
to accept the modest gifts set beside her,

I asked her to sweeten my bitter, burnt heart
with her sugar, a source of the finest honey.

She put down the harp and began to talk about poetry,
her every word was worth a whole pearl necklace.

She spoke of metre, rhyme and amphibology,
with fine expressions and elegant content.

I was stunned and amazed at the reasoning of that moon,
her speech was an embellishment for real connoisseurs.

After the sweet words of that moon and some wine,
the signs of drunkenness began to take over our heads.

Forgetting good and evil, I undid her dress,
and with my arms I made a belt for her buttocks.

I jumped up and swiftly sat between her thighs,
prey to desire, and got utterly carried away.

But what could I do, alas, my hare lay flat
like a drunk in the fumes of drunkenness.

I jumped upon her once more, tumbled and tried again,
but immobile, that hare didn't rise and I could do nothing.

Seeing my cock so limp, she leapt out
from underneath and soon got on top.

Resting there, she went up and down in great style,
but my one-eyed snake was now blind and also deaf.

She shook about above while it continued to sleep beneath,
and, for this, my soul suffered more than a thousand pains.

Greatly embarrassed, I said: 'O dear moon,
the desire for a boy has come to my cock.

It is not accustomed to being in the company of women,
it always keeps away from cunts and only looks for arses.'

She laughed and said: 'All right, you have a real cock,
and it wants to walk among mountains and slopes.'

She turned round and showed something similar to an arch,
as high as the stars, which cast a bright light into my eyes:

roses mixed with jasmine appeared,
two tulips wide open round a bud.

So I plunged into that posterior
with such force that my liver bled.

Only one vein, however, among all the others, didn't swell.
What can be said about this? What a miserable figure I cut!

When she saw my cock still lifeless,
she sent down a fart, made a great smell,

and covered me with shit from my pubes
to my knee: such shame sickened my soul.

I said to her: 'What have you done? What on earth is this?
O whore, why have you brought me such misfortune?'

She replied: 'Be off with you, you pansy of a poet!
I have seen that all you deserve is a donkey's cock!

What I've done is fitting for your beard,
all you have for a cock is a piece of wood!

To your great shame, you tied a belt in the middle
of your thighs. Only a belt and you call it your cock!'

She put her chador back on her head, did up her dress,
and left. This is what I wanted to tell you in poetry,

replying to the poem by Mir Mo'ezzi which begins with these words:
'Look at the moon newly risen midst the down of that beautiful boy!'[361]

Suzani

The second reply, this time by Pur-e Bahâ to Kamâl od-Din, is equally free and outrageous in content and is connected to the model, as the author states in the last line, by the desecrating contrast between the refrains. In this case, too, the two poems share the same metre and rhyme:

O idol, my cock has swollen again,
a fire has come to its restless head.

In longing for your rose-coloured buttocks,
my cock has become sharper than a thorn.

That disaster, my cock, is a constant obsession,
I hold it in my hand both by day and by night.

My cock has been shocked by passion,
shaken by bile, and its blood boiled up.

If my friend doesn't give me his arse, by force or begging,
my cock without its gold is tormented, laments and pines.

It's so swollen that its skin has broken,
my cock is so hard that it has burst.

This isn't a cock, it's a whale
famed with the name of cock.

With its head up in the air and its mouth full of foam,
my cock is like a raging camel that has broken its bridle.

If someone wants to embrace me, then my cock
jumps straight up between that person's thighs.

My cock is driven by passion and, like a falcon,
has two bells tightly bound to its feet for the hunt.

My cock drives me to promise money
to those silver-breasted rose-cheeked idols,

and, when inside their silken arses, my cock
is studded with gold like a blood-red brocade.[362]

Although I don't have the kingdom of Fereydun,[363]
my cock is for me like his heavy bull-headed sceptre.

Were Zahhâk to become my little slave, even for only a single night,
like a snake my cock would go into his arse and out of his shoulders.[364]

Rostam would never have taken his arse off his horse[365]
out of fear, if Esfandiyâr had had a cock similar to mine.[366]

If my cock went to war and fired off balls,
it would be capable of fucking any kingdom.

If I stuck this cock as strongly as a donkey up into the arse of a cow,
she would fall down to the ground for the pain in her navel and back.

From the time when my humble cock swelled up,
it has set arses alight and poured water in cunts.

And if you don't really believe what I am saying,
let me put my cock straight up behind your balls.

You have only two balls but, when my cock
is up you, it casts a spell and doubles them.

My powerful cock brings good fortune,
satisfying all the desires of everyone:

whoever has had my cock up their arse in the last year or two,
has become a noble and has gained many honours and wealth.

Now they are ministers, officials and even sovereigns,
those great dignitaries up whose arse I stuck my cock.

Carnelian and gold are assured to whosoever
takes from behind the mercury of my cock.

If I stuck my cock into the hole of a mountain,
every stone up there would become a red ruby.[367]

Two fists long and just as wide, it has a hat,
this is what my cock is in the eyes of the wise.

When it was circumcised it never moaned.
How well behaved and patient my cock is!

My cock loves arses above all but, out of pure spite,
it is also ready to ruin a cunt with its iron strokes.

My cock has become as hard as a rock for the following reason:
if a cunt commits adultery, my cock stones it to obey the law.[368]

When my cock swings about in the air like a snake's head,
every cunt will become as prickly as a porcupine out of fear.

Yesterday, without me having done anything,
a whore came and deceitfully asked for my cock.

I said to her: 'Your cunt is wide and cold' 'No, it's not so at all',
was her answer 'and if you don't believe me, bring your cock here!'

I replied: 'Don't talk shit and be off with you!
My cock has never had dealings with cunts!'

If the treasury of the arse were to levy taxes, then my cock
would be ready to pay a hundredfold more than other cocks.

But if cunts were to ask for a similar amount of taxes,
my cock would raise questions at the time of the reckoning.

Any time they want a champion to fight a cunt,
my cock is ready to be the leading horseman.

When my fiery cock welcomes an arse,
it offers food and drink in that great pot.

My cock dispenses pearls and gems from its ruby lips,
every time it uses the ring of an arse like an earring.

Since, like a candle, my cock put a fiery hat on its head,
it has been standing in silence, totally melted in tears.

The flames in plane trees come alight by themselves,
and that is the reason why this fire is in my cock![369]

The cock has never heard anywhere
such eloquent words depicting it.

Not even the best texts of anatomy
have described the cock so carefully.

Anvari and Suzani would lift their heads from the grave,
were they to hear the name of this famous cock of mine.[370]

If I lay my cock on the judge of Kirang's arse,[371]
his cock will surely try to intercede with mine.

To describe it, Suzani's poetry will suit well,
although he didn't have a cock of this kind.

The soul of Serâj-e Qomri congratulates me,
if I stick my cock up the arse of Kâmyâr's wife.

Before me, none of the best poets has ever used
the word 'cock' like this, in one line after another.

Kamâl used the word 'hand' as a refrain
in a *qaside*. Now my reply to him is: cock![372]

Pur-e Bahâ

Biographies of the Poets[373]

'Abbâsi He can probably be identified with Abu 'l 'Abbâs al-Fazl ebn-e 'Abbâs al-Rabenjâni, originally from Rabenjân, near Samarkand, a poet at the Samanid court who flourished in the first half of the 10th century and enjoyed considerable fame in his lifetime and over the following few centuries. Included in the *Loghat-e Fors* and other contemporary texts, only around a hundred of his lines have survived, some in a satirical vein. His style is characterised by both archaisms and simple direct expressions.

Abu 'l- 'Alâ' He was born in Ganja between 1096 and 1106. In some verses, he described himself as master and father-in-law of Khâqâni. He wrote for the Shirvanshah ruler Manuchehr, and was his poet laureate; he also helped Khâqâni to enter court circles. Relations between the two poets deteriorated so badly, however, that they even came to engage in fierce exchanges of obscene satirical poetry. Around a hundred lines of his poetry have survived. His probable date of death is 1160.

Abu 'Âsem We know very little about this poet, and only a few of his lines have come down to us. Two are included in the *Loghat-e Fors*, and so we can deduce that he was active at the beginnings of Persian poetry, probably around the turn of the 10th and 11th centuries.

Adib Sâber Active in the first half of the 12th century, he began his career in his native city of Termez, in Central Asia, before moving to Marv, then Balkh and, lastly, Chorasmia. Official panegyrist to the Saljuq ruler Sanjar, he also wrote poems in praise of the Khwarazmshah sovereign Atsiz. His poetry is characterised by simplicity and elegance and was admired by Anvari. His ghazals are particularly refined, and he was familiar with Arabic poetry and the rules of versification. Although devout, Adib Sâber nonetheless wrote satirical and obscene poetry, albeit less bold than that of his contemporaries Anvari, Sanâ'i and Suzani. He had a fierce poetic dispute with Vatvât. His much admired rich divan has survived. After thwarting an attack on Sanjar's life by Atsiz, he was drowned on the orders of the latter some time between 1143 and 1148.

Âgahi Originally from Khorasan, he lived in the age of the Timurid ruler Hoseyn Bâyqarâ (1469–1506). A well-educated and erudite poet, he composed *qaside* but was also fond of writing playful and obscene poetry.

ʿAmʿaq He was born in Bukhara, where he spent his childhood and lived in the late 11th and early 12th centuries. In 1068 he moved to Samarkand and the court of the Qarakhanid sovereign Shams ol-Molk Nasr, becoming his respected panegyrist. He had a famous dispute at court with his rival poet Rashidi. His son Hamid is said to have exchanged satirical poetry with the great Suzani. ʿAmʿaq often made clever use of rhetorical figures in elegant, fluent language. His poetical comparisons are particularly successful. He was greatly admired by his contemporaries, even by major poets such as Anvari and Suzani. The latter mentions him as an important writer of satirical poetry among his predecessors. In addition to the two poems translated here, we have not found other passages of this kind. In the *tazkere* they claim that when the daughter of the Saljuq sultan Sanjar died in 1130, the ruler invited the by then elderly and blind poet to write the funerary elegy. Around 600 lines have survived from his divan and include *qaside*, *robâʿi* and *qetʿe*. According to some sources, he lived to a very old age and probably died around 1149.

ʿAmmâre Born in Marv, he lived in the late 10th and early 11th centuries and was active at both the Samanid and Ghaznavid courts. We can deduce from some sources that he was still alive in 1005 and that he spent his whole life in his native city. His around one hundred surviving lines are all characterised by clarity and elegance. The fact that many of his lines are in the *Loghat-e Fors* and other 11th-century dictionaries testifies to his reputation at that time. His obscene verse is particularly scurrilous.

Anvari One of the great Persian poets, he lived and wrote in the 12th century. He was born at Abivard, in Khorasan, at an unknown date. Many of the details of his life mentioned in the sources are not very reliable historically (for example, he was described as having squandered his father's wealth but also as a devout student of religious matters). He arrived at the Saljuq court of Sanjar around 1135 and stayed on as a panegyrist there until the death of the sovereign in 1157. In any case he also wrote poetry in praise of many other important people. He appears to have spent some years in Balkh. During the military campaign against the Khwarazmshah sultan Atsiz, he exchanged invective poems with the poet laureate at that court, Vatvât. He wrote *qaside*, ghazals, *robâʿi* and *qetʿe* but his fame rests mainly on his *qaside* and *qetʿe*. Anvari is considered to be an erudite poet (hence his title of Hakim/'Wise Man'), and his poetry often features terms and themes from various disciplines (logic, music, astronomy, mathematics, metaphysics, religious law and natural sciences). His *qaside* are very complex, rich in Arabic words and often difficult to interpret. Indeed commentaries have been written for his most difficult lines. He is famed for his elaborate metaphors. Sometimes, however, especially in the ghazals, his language is close to everyday use. Many of his compositions have been included in anthologies and texts on rhetoric, proof that his work was important and influential. Most critics consider Anvari to be the greatest panegyrist in Persian poetry, but he also wrote many fierce invectives against a wide range of people, which led to him being acknowledged as one of the founders of Persian satirical poetry. Because of this fame, some poetic attacks, including a short poem on Balkh, were falsely attributed to him, which made him a laughing stock in the streets of the city. Highly irascible, he wrote in a satirical and obscene vein, specially in the *qetʿe* and partly in the *robâʿi*; some manuscripts include an incomplete *masnavi* entitled *Hajv-e Qâzi-ye Kirang*. The language in these texts is very rich, creative and at times particularly scurrilous. Some critics describe him as the most audacious writer in Persian literature, after his contemporary Suzani (to whom he refers explicitly in his poetry). His satire was often directed against the corrupt customs of the age. In his last years he is said to have abandoned writing poetry in favour of a quiet life of solitude. In a famous quatrain, Jâmi calls him, together with Ferdowsi and Saʿdi, one of the 'three prophets' of Persian poetry. He died in Balkh, at an uncertain date for which there are various suggestions (1160/1, 1169/70, 1186).

ʿÂref-e Ardabili He was born in Ardabil, in the north-west of Iran, around 1311. He went to the Shirvanshah court at the bidding of the sovereign Key Kâ'us ebn-e Key Qobâd, and became his son's tutor. He wrote a *masnavi* entitled *Farhâdnâme* in which he retold in desecrating tones the story of Farhâd narrated in the *Khosrow o Shirin* by Nezâmi-ye Ganjavi and at the same time praised Key Kâ'us and his son Hushang. The text seems to have been begun at the Shirvanshah court and completed on the poet's return to Ardabil. One feature of this *masnavi* is the description of carnal relations, while there is also an interesting use of words borrowed from local dialects. His date of death is not known, but he lived for over 70 years.

Asir od-Din-e Akhsikati He was originally from Akhsikat, the chief city in the central Asian region of Ferghana. Around 1153 he emigrated to the court of the Saljuq sultans in western Iran and other principalities in those regions. He wrote *qaside* for the Saljuq Alp Arslân and for the Ildeguzid Qezel Arslân, among others. At the court of Qezel Arslân, he is said to have taken over as poet laureate from Mojir od-Din. He had some famous poetic disputes with the latter and also with Khâqâni. He had no scruples about using scurrilous words. An erudite and innovative poet, he was considered a great writer of *qaside* and was particularly clever in his use of refrains. He also wrote some elegant ghazals. His date of death is not certain (some suggest 1181, 1183 or 1211).

ʿAsjadi Originally from Marv (or, according to some sources, Herat), he lived in the late 10th and the first half of the 11th centuries. He wrote for Ghaznavid rulers and was a companion at court of two other great poets, ʿOnsori (some believe ʿAsjadi was his student) and Farrokhi. A prolific author and one of the first to focus on a wide use of rhetorical figures, ʿAsjadi was admired for his encomiastic poetry, lyrics and also satirical verse, in which at times he used a very scurrilous vocabulary. Around 200 of his lines have come down to us, preserved in anthologies and dictionaries.

ʿAttâr Born in Nishapur, Khorasan, around 1145, he is one of the most celebrated mystic Persian poets. There is very little reliable information about his life. He not only studied Arabic and religion but also medicine and had inherited from his father the profession of apothecary, which guaranteed him a living without having to work as a panegyrist. He travelled a good deal. His literary output was not very well known in his lifetime and his greatness as a poet and mystic was appreciated only from the 15th century on. There are many doubts, however, concerning the authenticity of all the works attributed to him. He wrote ghazals, *robâʿi* and *qaside*, even though he was not really a court poet. His greatest fame, however, is due to some *masnavi*, the best-known being the *Manteq ot-Teyr*, a masterpiece of Persian literature. ʿAttâr's poetic thinking focused on various aspects of the Sufi world, and its theoretical, practical and educational aspects. His production was a source of inspiration for the other great mystic poet, Rumi. ʿAttâr also wrote the text entitled *Tazkerat ol-Owliyâʾ*, consisting of biographies of the most important Sufi masters. In his criticism of certain aspects of social life, he did not resort to bold or obscene language. He died in 1221 during the Mongolian invasion of his native city, Nishapur.

Bâbâ Sowdâ'i Originally from Abivard, Khorasan, and active in the 15th century, his first pen-name was Khâvari, which then changed to Sowdâ'i ('The Mad Man') after he had gone out of his mind during a period spent in the desert and mountains. He wrote *qaside* in praise of the Timurid prince Bâysonqor (1397–1433). He also composed ghazals and verse of social criticism. His compositions often had the accents typical of *hazl* poetry. He died at the age of about 90 in around 1449.

Badr-e Jâjarmi Born at Jâjarm, north Khorasan, at an unknown date, he moved to Isfahan, where he was received as a poet at the court of the governor Shams od-Din Mohammad-e Joveyni and his son Bahâ od-Din, for whom he wrote *qaside*. He also wrote in praise of another member of the family, the historian 'Atâ Malek-e Joveyni. Although his poems reveal great technical and rhetorical skills, they were never considered examples of good poetry. His son Mohammad (known by the name of Jâjarmi) wrote the *Mo'nes ol-Ahrâr fi Daqâ'eq ol-Ash'âr*, an important source for contemporary poets and containing works by Badr-e Jâjarmi himself, who died in 1287.

Boshâq He was born in Shiraz, probably in the second half of the 14th century, and attended the Timurid court. As can be evinced from his title (Hallâj), he worked in the cotton business. He used traditional forms to express critical and playful content and is famous for his satirical poems devoted to the gastronomical world. His poems include imitations of classical poets, such as Hâfez, Sa'di and Salmân. He was greatly influenced by 'Obeyd's satirical style but refrained from using his obscene language. He died in 1423 or 1427.

Dibâji Born in Samarkand, he lived in the 11th century and, according to some scholars, was active at the Ganja court of the Shaddadid rulers (others claim, on the other hand, that he was active the Ravvadid court in Azerbaijan). He had a shrewd, witty nature, but we have no further information about him. Only a dozen of his lines have survived.

Ebn-e Khatib Also known as Pur-e Khatib, he was the 'son of a preacher' (this is the meaning of both variants of his pseudonym, while his first name was Ahmad) from the city of Ganja. Since he was celebrated as the companion of the poetess Mahsati, he must have lived in the 12th century. With Mahsati he was involved in a famous love affair, characterised by outrageous aspects and exchanges of satirical poems, narrated in a text of uncertain date but 14th century.

Ebn-e Yamin Born into a family of landowners at Faryumad, western Khorasan, in 1286/7, he found employment at various courts (especially the Âl-e Kart court in Herat), and was thus a witness to the power struggle that beset Khorasan at the time. He was a man of great moral and religious virtue. His divan includes all the major poetic genres, but he was one of the acknowledged masters of the *qet'e*. He wrote both in Arabic and Persian and his compositions are generally simple and clear, but already reveal the syntactic complexities and the typical Arabicisms of the following centuries. He wrote some satirical and playful poetry, also resorting to scurrilous language. He lost the only manuscript of his divan during a battle, and so was forced to redraft it later. In the last years of his life he returned to his birthplace of Faryumad, where he died in 1368.

Farghâni He was a Sufi poet, originally from the region of Ferghana, in Central Asia. The little information we have about his life comes from his own divan. Active in the 13th century, he was forced to leave his region during the Mongolian invasion, settling first in Tabriz and later in Asia Minor. Neglected for several centuries, his verse mainly consist of poems in praise of the Lord and the prophet Muhammad. His dates of birth and death are unknown.

Gorgâni He was originally from the Caspian region of Gorgân. Little is known about his life and the information all comes from his *masnavi* entitled *Vis o Râmin*, composed around 1055. He moved to Isfahan after the city was conquered by the Saljuq Toghril and lived under the protection of the new governor Abu 'l-Fath Mozaffar, to whom he dedicated *Vis o Râmin*. This *masnavi* was often the subject of local censure, because it describes, without condemning, adultery committed by a woman, the princess Vis.

Hâfez Traditionally considered to be the greatest Persian poet, he was born in Shiraz, in the heart of the Iranian plateau around 1320. Despite his great popularity, there is very little firm information about his life. The sources do agree, however, about his name: Shams od-Din Mohammad. His pen-name, Hâfez, is due to the fact that he knew the Koran off by heart. He rarely and reluctantly left his native city. He is once said to have gone to the Persian Gulf to embark on a ship for India, but terrified at the sight of the sea, he immediately went back to Shiraz. His *qaside* reflect the political instability of the period and are dedicated to various local dynasties: the Injuids, Muzaffarids and the Jalayirids. Hâfez is greatly loved at home and much admired in the Western world (Goethe, in his *West-Eastern Divan*, described him as his 'twin'). He is famed for his ghazals, in which earthly passion and mystical reflection are often inextricably combined to give rise to a perfect blend of sensible and supersensible elements to the background of great wisdom. In this context, in his divan we can find a wide range of feelings and sensations of both a religious and profane type, expressed through the filter of the fashionable canon. Significantly, the two titles most frequently attributed to him are Lesân ol-Gheyb ('The Language of the Unknown') and Tarjomân ol-Asrâr ('The Interpreter of Secrets'). His poems show a learned and harmonious plurality of themes described in elegant language. Some of his compositions are severe critiques of the hypocritical and corrupt behaviour of the religious authorities and Sufis of his day, expressed in refined and subtle ways, often also ironic. He died in Shiraz around 1390.

Homâm A poet in the Ilkhanid period, we have no information about his birth (probably around 1238) and initial career. At a mature age he was a politician and poet at Tabriz. He is mainly famed for his ghazals, which he composed by emulating the content and style of Sa'di, and in fact he was known as the Sa'di of Azerbaijan. He also wrote some *masnavi*, one of which takes as a model Sanâ'i' *Hadiqat ol-Haqiqe*. He was admired by various later poets, including 'Obeyd and Hâfez. He died in 1314.

Jamâl od-Din He flourished in the second half of the 12th century. Almost all the biographical information about him is derived from his divan. He was born in Isfahan, where he had a religious upbringing and spent much of his life. Initially he seems to have worked as a painter and gilder in the Isfahan bazaar. He wrote his first *qaside* in 1160 and his last in 1187/8. Apart from some poems in praise of Saljuq and Bavandid rulers, most of his *qaside* were for local dignitaries in Isfahan. He had four children. One of them, Kamâl od-Din, also became a poet and achieved greater fame than his father. Besides *qaside*, written in a very straightforward style, Jamâl od-Din composed particularly elegant ghazals, *tarkibband* (strophic poem), *robâ'i* and *qet'e*. His poems were addressed not only to rulers and political personages but also poets, such as Vatvât, Khâqâni and Mojir od-Din (with the latter two he had disputes). He was a successful author of satires, mainly written in the form of the *qet'e*. He acknowledged his indebtedness to Anvari. According to some sources, he probably died not long before 1202/3.

Jâmi A celebrated poet and mystic, he is one of the great writers of Persian literature. He was born in Kharjerd, between Mashhad and Herat, in 1414, but adopted his pen-name from the nearby village of Jâm. He soon moved to Herat and then Samarkand, where he completed his studies, revealing his great talent and a prodigious memory. Following a spiritual crisis, he took the mystical way and associated with the Sufi in the order of the Naqshbandiyya. He entered the service of the Timurids and had close relations with the sovereign Hoseyn Bayqarâ and his counsellor and minister ʿAli Shir Navâʾi. After a pilgrimage to Mecca, he returned to Herat in 1474, establishing increasingly good relations with the court circles. Significantly, ʿAli Shir Navâʾi became a member of the Naqshbandiyya, of which Jâmi was the spiritual leader at the time. In the last years of his life, he enjoyed great prestige, even though he continued to lead a modest life in the country. Jâmi was a prolific author and wrote in both Arabic and Persian. His vast divan includes *qaside*, ghazals, *robâʿi* and *qetʿe*. His seven *masnavi* are known under the name of *Haft Owrang*. Another of his major works is the *Bahârestân*, a mixture of prose and poetry written following the model of Saʿdi's *Golestân*. The sixth chapter contains many light-hearted anecdotes, some obscene. He also drafted prose treatises, including many on religious and theological themes. Among his other writings are a text on music, grammatical compendia and short studies dedicated to rhyme, metre and the genre of the enigma. As a mystic, he combined the theories of the Arab philosopher and poet Ibn ʿArabi (1165–1240) with the Persian literary tradition. Some 19th-century critics gave him the title of Khâtam osh-Shoʿarâ ('Seal of Poets'), thus acknowledging him as the last great representative of the classical tradition. He died in Herat in 1492. At the time he was the most celebrated writer of the Persian language, widely esteemed from India to Turkey.

Kâferak He was born in Ghazna and wrote poetry in the 11th century, probably during the reign of the Ghaznavid Ebrâhim. Only a dozen of his poems survive, all on satirical and obscene subjects and also with scurrilous terms. He was famed and feared for his verbal attacks.

Kamâl od-Din He was active in Isfahan in the late 12th and early 13th centuries. Born around 1172, he succeeded his father, Jamâl od-Din, as panegyrist of the Hanafite judge Rokn od-Din Sâʿed and subsequently his son. He wrote many *qaside* for other personages, including the Khwarazmshah rulers who, having defeated the Saljuqs, became the lords of Isfahan. Kamâl od-Din was very skilled not only in inventing new images and meanings (hence his title: Khallâq ol-Maʿâni/'Creator of Thoughts') but also in the use of complex refrains. Besides *qaside*, he wrote much admired ghazals and many satires especially in the *qetʿe* form (many of them were protests against his patrons and at times in scurrilous terms), in which he shows his notable verse-making skills. He also wrote religious poems and a brief treatise in Arabic. Given his skill, he was often compared to Anvari. In old age he retired from court life. According to some sources, he was killed by the Mongols in 1237, after they had occupied Isfahan.

Kesâ'i He was born in 953, as he himself states in a poem from which we can also deduce that he was still alive in 1000/1. He was very probably originally from Marv, where he spent most of his life in the service, first of the Samanid and then the Ghaznavid rulers. He wrote very competently both in Arabic and Persian and composed encomiastic, lyrical and didactic poems, but was known above all as a religious poet. His poems about nature reveal a special sensibility. A number of his compositions have survived, as well as a series of fragments, some recorded in the *Loghat-e Fors*. His date of death is unknown.

Khâju He was born in Kerman in 1290. After various journeys, he returned to Iran in around 1335 and settled in Shiraz. He tried to obtain a position at court by dedicating *qaside* to the rulers of contemporary dynasties: the Ilkhanids, Muzaffarids and Injuids. He also cultivated important relations with the religious authorities and Sufi masters. His work undoubtedly exercised an influence on the formation of Hâfez. He composed *qaside*, *robâ'i* and, especially, ghazals. Following the example of Nezâmi-ye Ganjavi, he was one of the first poets to write a *Khamse*, i.e. a set of five *masnavi*. Critics are not unanimous in their assessment of his poetry, but he undeniably played an important role in the history of Persian literature. He died in Shiraz around 1349.

Khâqâni A major Persian poet, he was born in the Caucasian region historically known as Shervân in around 1127. Of modest origins (his mother was a cook and his father a carpenter, opposed to his decision to become a poet) he was brought up and educated by his uncle in various disciplines after his father had died. He thus became an erudite poet at an early age, admired for his powerful imagination and rhetorical devices. His very unusual knowledge of the Christian tradition was due to the Nestorian origins of his mother and the specific syncretic milieu (Christian-Islamic) of the places where he trained. His language is very precise and often inspired by the scientific world. Khâqâni's poems are so difficult that from the 15th century on explicative commentaries have been written for his more complex lines. He also wrote in Arabic and had a great influence over later poets, even the great Nezâmi-ye Ganjavi; his texts were included in many *tazkere*. He wrote *qaside*, ghazals, *tar-*

ji'band, robâ'i, qet'e, a celebrated *masnavi* entitled *Tohfat ol-'Erâqeyn* and a series of letters. His fame is principally due to his *qaside*, some also non-panegyrical and many characterised by the presence of a refrain. He wrote poems of praise principally to the Shirvanshah rulers, and especially to Manuchehr and his son Akhsetân; for most of his life he resided in their capital, Shamakha. He also dedicated various compositions to other powerful figures. Conceited and irascible, he wrote at times virulent poetic attacks on a wide range of people: Abu 'l-'Alâ' and Mojir od-Din (according to some sources, the former was his master and father-in-law and the latter his student), his poet contemporaries (Vatvât and Asir od-Din-e Akhsikati), a master from the past like 'Onsori, his father, wife, daughters, political and religious representatives and the women of Baghdad. He mainly expressed his satire in *qet'e* and partly in *robâ'i*. He also excelled in the literary genre of the *habsiyyât*, poetry associated with imprisonment, which he had himself suffered. He died in Tabriz some time between 1186 and 1199.

Labibi Very probably originally from Khorasan, he lived in the late 10th and first half of the 11th centuries. According to some historians, he was active at the courts both of the Âl-e Mohtâj of Chaghâniyân and of the Ghaznavids. Some of his compositions in a fine style and various fragments have survived (a total of around 200 lines). The fragments are often invectives and in many cases contain scurrilous terms. As evidence of his popularity with later poets, we can point to one of his poems that inspired a *qaside* by Mas'ud-e Sa'd.

Lâme'i Originally from the Caspian region of Gorgân, he lived in the 11th century. We have very little information about his life. He seems, however, to have been in the service of Saljuq rulers, including Toghril and Alp Arslân. His poems have a simple elegant style and follow the example of the great poets of the Khorasanian style: 'Onsori, Farrokhi and Manuchehri. Around one thousand of his lines have survived.

Mahsati Midway between legend and historical reality, she has been described in a great variety of terms: erudite, courtesan, dissolute, musician, singer, poetess and scribe. She is thought to have originally been from Ganja and lived in the 12th century, and as such was one of the first poetesses writing in Persian. In his *Elâhinâme*, 'Attâr mentions her as a woman close to the Saljuq king Sanjar (she is also said to have been his mistress); others claim that Mahsati lived in the 11th century, at the Ghaznavid court of Mahmud. Numerous *robâ'i* (around 250) have been attributed to her, many on sentimental subjects and some obscene. Mahsati was the main character in a famous love story narrated in a text of uncertain date but 14th century, in which she is depicted as a woman who frequents the taverns in the outskirts of Ganja and who exchanges outrageous lines with her lover, Ebn-e Khatib.

Manuchehri He was born in Dâmghân, to the south-east of the Caspian Sea, in around 1000. An important panegyrist at the Ghaznavid court, he was a leading exponent, together with ʿOnsori and Farrokhi, of the so-called Khorasanian style, the first style of Persian poetry. He is credited with the invention of the *mosammat*, a strophic composition. He had a strong predilection for pre-Islamic Arabic poetry and at times sought to imitate it. He showed a special interest in describing vivid, dynamic details. He died in around 1040.

Maʿrufi Originally from Balkh, he lived in the 10th century and was active at the Samanid court. We have no information about his life. Only a few dozen of his lines have survived in anthologies and dictionaries, including the *Loghat-e Fors*. Some of these lines are satirical and obscene.

Masʿud-e Saʿd He was born around 1046 in Lahore, where his father, originally from Hamadân, had moved to enter service with the Ghaznavid rulers. He was the first major Indo-Persian poet, admired by other poets, such as Mokhtâri and Sanâʾi. His poetic career was linked to the Ghaznavid campaigns of expansion in India. Having fallen into disgrace at court, he spent several years in prison. He was then pardoned and became the court librarian at Ghazna. His poetry follows the classical canon of the early poets but also has some innovative features: besides the moving *habsiyyât*, he wrote works on days and months of the year and *shahrâshub* dedicated to young artisans in the city, which were among the earliest examples of this genre. He composed only a few lines of satirical and obscene verse. He died in 1121/2.

Mojir od-Din He was born in Beylaqân, a city in the Caucasian region, and was active in the 12th century. Some sources claim he was a student of Khâqâni, to whom he addressed some poems (both praise and satire). He wrote *qaside* for Shirvanshah, Ildeguzid and Saljuq rulers. He was at the centre of a diatribe concerning Isfahan: after writing some lines criticising the city, he received replies from various local poets, including obscene poetry by Jamâl od-Din. Mojir od-Din's satirical lines on Isfahan were initially attributed to Khâqâni, who confuted the accusation in verse. Mojir od-Din is celebrated for his extreme formal sophistication (see, for example, his lines written using only letters with no diacritic signs). At times, however he uses clear, fluent language. He wrote just a few satirical and obscene poems. He also wrote poetry while in prison. He was murdered in obscure circumstances in around 1197.

Mokhtâri Originally from Ghazna, he flourished as a poet in the late 11th and first half of the 12th centuries. A panegyrist, especially of the Ghaznavid ruler Mas'ud III, he then fell into disgrace and moved to the Saljuq court at Kerman, but eventually returned to the Ghaznavid court. He also wrote *qaside* for the last Buyid rulers. In his later years he went to the Qarakhanid court in Samarkand. He was esteemed by Sanâ'i and wrote lines in honour of Mas'ud-e Sa'd. His few satirical and obscene lines were not greatly admired. Two dates have been suggested for his death: 1149 and 1159.

Monjik Active in the second half of the 10th century, he wrote *qaside* at the court of the Âl-e Mohtâj ruling in the region of Chaghâniyân, to the north of Termez, his birthplace in Central Asia. After the fall of the Âl-e Mohtâj, according to some sources, he joined the Ghaznavid court. His around 300 surviving lines are generally characterised by a distinct elegance and considerable inventive power. His divan became famous in the following centuries. His many satirical and obscene lines (around 80 have survived) were considered to be the best of his age and include both social criticism and personal diatribes. The importance of this production is mentioned by Suzani, the great master of the genre. Monjik is one of the most often cited poets in the *Loghat-e Fors*. He was also an esteemed musician.

Morâdi Originally from Bukhara, he lived in the 10th century and was active at the Samanid court. We know nothing of his life and only a few of his lines have survived. He mainly wrote in Arabic. Rudaki wrote an elegy to commemorate his death.

Nâser-e Khosrow A poet, philosopher and celebrated traveller, he was born at Qobâdiyân in the region of Marv in 1004. He studied various disciplines and several languages. He initially worked as a secretary for some local princes and then, inspired by some visions, set off on a long journey, which he described in his *Safarnâme*. In Egypt he became a fervent follower of Ismailism. He wrote religious and philosophical texts and a divan also mainly consisting of religious and philosophical poems. He spent the last part of his life in exile in the Badakhshân mountains, where he died sometime between 1072 and 1077.

Nezâmi-ye 'Aruzi Born in Samarkand around the end of the 11th century, he wrote a celebrated work called *Chahâr Maqâle* (between 1155 and 1157), a text on four professions (secretary, poet, astronomer and physician), which is very important for knowledge of many aspects—not just literary—of the contemporary culture. This same work provides us with the little information that we have about his life. He worked at the Ghurid court and met some of the great poets of the age, such as ʿOmar Khayyâm and Moʿezzi. Very few of his lines have survived. Not of great literary value, they are mainly satirical and also obscene.

Nezâmi-ye Ganjavi He was born in 1141 at Ganja, now in Azerbaijan but at the time mainly inhabited by people of Iranian origins. Little information has come down to us about his life. His mother was of Kurdish origin and died prematurely. He received a very broad education and mastered various disciplines. He is mainly famed for his celebrated quintet, *Khamse*, consisting of five *masnavi*: *Makhzan ol-Asrâr*, *Khosrow o Shirin*, *Haft Peykar*, *Leylâ o Majnun* and *Eskandarnâme*. He also composed ghazals and *qaside*, mostly now lost. Although his works are dedicated to rulers, he was not a proper court poet. He was renowned for his powerful imagination, mastery of language, narrative skills, understanding of society and deep religious feeling. He exercised a great influence over subsequent developments in the history of Persian literature. His poetic production was a source for various imitations and inspired paintings by many miniaturists. He died in 1209.

Nezâri Born at Birjand, Khorasan, around 1247, he was one of the most important poets in the late 13th and early 14th centuries. An Ismailist, he wrote *qaside* for the rulers of the Âl-e Kart dynasty. His rich, varied divan includes not only *qaside*, but also ghazals, *qetʿe* and *masnavi*. He often criticised the hypocrisy of his age and defended the weaker classes. He admired and imitated poets such as Khâqâni and Saʿdi. After several journeys (Isfahan, Tabriz, Caucasus, etc.), he returned to his native region, where he died in around 1321.

ʿObeyd Also known as Zâkâni, he is the greatest satirical poet in Persian literature. He was born at Zâkân, a town near Qazvin, a few years before 1319. His well-educated family was closely associated with the administrative apparatus. As a young man, he held public office for several years. When the Ilkhanid kingdom fell, he moved to Shiraz, where he was active at the court of Abu Eshâq Inju, for whom he wrote many *qaside*. When that ruler was defeated and killed by the Muzaffarid sovereign Mobârez od-Din Mohammad in 1357, ʿObeyd fled Shiraz and was to return only in the reign of Shâh Shojâʿ, to whom he dedicated several poems. Like Abu Eshâq Inju, Shâh Shojâʿ was a patron of Hâfez, but there is no evidence suggesting that the two poets knew each other. While staying in Baghdad, he composed some poems in praise of the Jalayirid ruler Sheikh Oveys. ʿObeyd wrote serious and comic works, but his fame is mainly due to the latter: satirical and obscene works both in verse and prose. They marked the transition from the invective *ad personam*, typical of Suzani and other poets in the Saljuq age, to criticism of a more political and social nature. Among other things, he condemned despotism, hypocrisy, religious intolerance, the malfunctioning of the legal system, immorality of all kinds and various forms of cultural backwardness (without, however, distancing himself from the deep-rooted misogyny of his age). These compositions, usually in a clear, elegant style, at times are in outrageous, scurrilous language. He also made many parodies of poems by other poets. He was well versed in Arabic and often demonstrated his broad knowledge in various sciences and disciplines. His works include the *Akhlâq ol-Ashrâf*, the *Resâla-ye Dah Fasl*, the *Resâla-ye Delgoshâ*, the *Resâla-ye Sad Pand*, the *Maktub-e Qalandarân* and the *Rishnâme*. He probably died in around 1370. Despite his great popularity, ʿObeyd was long neglected by the critics, especially because of his outrageous aspects, and only recently have his works been translated and adequately studied.

ʿOmar Khayyâm Born in Nishapur, Khorasan, in around 1048, he was a celebrated mathematician, astronomer, philosopher and poet. The Saljuq ruler Malek Shâh commissioned him to undertake a major reform of the calendar. His famous *robâʿi*, whose authenticity is widely debated, combine philosophical and mystical reflections with hedonistic and sceptical ideas. Edward Fitzgerald made a celebrated translation of ʿOmar Khayyâm's *robâʿi* in the 19th century. His probable date of death is around 1131.

Owhadi He was born in Marâghe, north-west Iran, in around 1274/5. His most important work is the *masnavi Jâm-e Jam*, modelled on Sanâ'i's *Hadiqat ol-Haqiqe* and dedicated to the Ilkhanid ruler Abu Saʿid. Besides mysticism, Owhadi was also notably interested in social and educational issues, which led him to be involved in town planning and schooling. Some critics believe his ghazals are not inferior to those of Hâfez. He is famed for his elegies. After a few journeys, he returned to his native city of Marâghe, where he died in 1338.

Pur-e Bahâ Also known under the name of Ebn-e Bahâ, he was originally from Jâm, a town between Mashhad and Herat, and lived in the 13th century, at the beginning of the Ilkhanid period. Very little is known about his life. His father was a judge, but Pur-e Bahâ chose a career as a poet. Having grown up in Khorasan, and especially in Herat, where he wrote poems in honour of the local governors, he then went to Azerbaijan, Isfahan and Baghdad. He composed *qaside* for various personages at the Ilkhanid court. His fame mainly rests on his satirical and obscene poetry, at times attacking corrupt rulers and the clergy. In this kind of production, he considered himself to be a disciple of Suzani. His poems on the male member are celebrated, and he liked to write playful replies to *qaside* by important poets, such as Sanâ'i and Nezâmi-ye Ganjavi. One special feature of his poetry is the use of Mongolian and Turkish words. He also knew Arabic. Some studies (Hoffmann 1990 and the entry in *Encyclopædia Iranica* 1982–) attribute to him a *masnavi* entitled *Kârnâme-ye Owqâf*, where he criticises and mocks the abuses of power and vices of the administrators in the pious foundations of Khâf. It is not clear where he spent the last part of his life, before his death in around 1284.

Qamar We know very little about his life. He was originally from Isfahan and was probably born in around 1155. He mainly wrote *qaside*, in the style of the ancient poets. His poems are important from the lexical point of view, since they contain references to various disciplines (botany, medicine, astronomy and philosophy) and everyday customs and practice. He composed *qaside* for the Salgurid sovereigns and eulogies to some powerful religious families in Isfahan. He also wrote satires and playful verse. He probably died between 1202 and 1217.

Qari Originally from Yazd, he lived in Shiraz in the second half of the 15th century. He is famed for his satirical poems devoted to the sartorial world. Many of them were written as imitations of poems by celebrated poets, including Hâfez.

Qomri There is very little information about him. He was born in around 1164 or 1184, probably in Âmol, Mâzanderân, as suggested by the fact that many of his *qaside* are addressed to princes in that region. After a period spent in Mâzanderân, he seems to have gone to Ray, and then Khorasan before eventually settling at the Khwarazmshah court. His style is reminiscent of Anvari's erudite manner. He was particularly skilled in the use of new compounds and complex refrains. He wrote in Arabic and Persian. Many of his works, especially the *qet'e* and *qaside*, are satirical and evoke the audacious, obscene spirit of Anvari and Suzani. He wrote a celebrated playful *masnavi* entitled *Kârnâme* (a clear allusion to his model, the *Kârnâme-ye Balkh* by Sanâ'i). In old age, he is said to have ceased writing outrageous and satirical poems. His probable year of death is 1227.

Rashidi Originally from Samarkand, he was active in the 12th century in Transoxiana, writing *qaside* at the Qarakhanid and Saljuq courts. He was particularly skilled in using rhetorical figures as regards both form and content. He is known to have engaged in poetic disputes with ʿAmʿaq and Masʿud-e Saʿd.

Rudaki He was the first great Persian poet, active in the 10th century. As his name suggests, he was originally from the village of Rudak, near Samarkand. He was active at the Samanid court. He was also a court singer and musician. Some whole poems and many scattered lines have survived from his rich divan. He is the most often cited author in the *Loghat-e Fors*. He laid the foundations for the so-called Khorasanian style, the earliest style of Persian poetry, and excelled in both panegyrical and lyrical poems, at times characterised by great simplicity. His few satirical and obscene lines are moderate in tone. His poetry enjoyed great fame for at least two centuries and its power is attested to by a famous episode: one of his compositions is said to have convinced the prince Samanid Nasr II to return to Bukhara and abandon the pleasures of his country retreat at Herat. At the end of his life, Rudaki fell into disgrace, having also lost his sight (although some claim he was blind from birth). His probable date of death is around 940.

Ruhi Originally from Valvâlej, near Balkh, he lived at the Saljuq court in the 12th century. In his verse he mentions Farrokhi, Masʿud-e Saʿd and Qatrân (some say the last was his master). His fame as a satirical and obscene author was so great that, according to an anecdote fashionable in his age, he only had to move his lips—even if he were about to pronounce the name of God—for everyone to fear they would be the butt of his poetic attacks. He earned the pseudonym of Kun-e Mardom ('People's Arse') for having mentioned in verse that the posterior was his favourite part of other people's bodies. His qualities as a serious poet, however, were also acknowledged and admired. Only a few of his lines have survived.

Rumi Known as Mowlavi or Mowlânâ, he is a great mystical poet and one of the masters of Persian poetry. He was born into a family with erudite traditions in Balkh in 1207. His father was a well-known preacher. Fear of the Mongols and various controversies induced the family to leave Balkh and move to Konya, Turkey, in around 1222. Here he became closely involved with mystical circles, and when the dervish Shams od-Din Mohammad-e Tabrizi arrived in Konya in 1244, Rumi became a fervent follower. After the dervish left the city, the poet was so enthusiastic about him that he adopted Shams-e Tabrizi as a pen-name in memory of his beloved master, and thus in a certain sense became identified with him. Rumi is said to have composed his poems when in a mystical trance. He left a rich divan of poems often simple and direct in tone, but especially the *Masnavi-ye Ma'navi*, a kind of compendium of Sufism, also known as the Persian Koran. Some of the spiritual messages in this text are illustrated in obscene anecdotes, since Rumi was convinced that these kinds of stories could help spread his work. This means that the passages concerned in the *Masnavi-ye Ma'navi* are a singular mixture of the sacred and the profane. He died in Konya in 1273. His funeral was attended by Muslims, Christians and Jews, evidence of his open mind and tolerance. His spiritual legacy has been kept alive by a confraternity of dervishes who practise ritual dances and are inspired by his teachings.

Sa'di He is a major figure in Persian literature. There are only a few firm details about his biography. Born in Shiraz some time between 1213 and 1219, he moved to Baghdad, where he studied at the celebrated Nezâmiyye. He subsequently undertook many journeys but became famed as a poet only when he returned to Shiraz in 1256/7 and composed the *Bustân* and the *Golestân*, dedicated to the local rulers. His interests lay not so much in theoretical speculations as in the observation of everyday life and its attendant teachings. Especially in the *Golestân*, a work of both prose and verse, his deep experience of earthly matters emerges along with his very understanding and tolerant spirit. He also wrote *qaside* and ghazals. Composed to earn him a living, the *qaside* suffer at times from a certain verbosity and repetitiveness, whereas the ghazals, often simple and musical, are some of the first accomplished examples of that melding of the sacred and the profane, or spiritual love and earthly passion, that was to pave the way to Hâfez's ghazal. A hallmark of his style is the so-called *sahl-e momtane'* ('inimitable facility'). His works include—although there are no definitive critical studies on the subject—several playful and obscene compositions gathered in a collection which goes under various titles: *Khabisât*, *Majâles ol-Hazl*, *Mazâhekât* and *Motâyyebât*. There are also facetious lines by him in the *Golestân*. Some of his satires are directed at the corrupt mores of the age. In a celebrated quatrain, Jâmi describes Sa'di, together with Anvari and Ferdowsi, as the three 'prophets' of Persian poetry. He was famed and greatly loved in his lifetime. He died in 1292, and his tomb in Shiraz is still often visited and venerated.

Salmân He was born in Sâve, in central-north Iran, in around 1300. He mainly sang the praise of the Jalayirids, and his *qaside* were among the last of the classical tradition. He also wrote ghazals and some *masnavi* on epic and love themes. His production reveals a solid technical and cultural background rather than true poetic inspiration. His most famous works include his *qaside-ye masnu'*, poems rich in rhetorical expedients. Some of his ghazals are reminiscent of those of Hâfez. He died in Sâve in around 1376.

Sanâ'i A great religious poet and one of the masters of Persian poetry, he was born in Ghazna, very probably in around 1087. At the beginning of his career, he wrote eulogies to some dignitaries at the Ghaznavid court. He was in contact with the poets Mas'ud-e Sa'd and Mokhtâri. Before the end of the reign of the Ghaznavid ruler Mas'ud III, he left for Balkh, where he wrote the *Kârnâme-ye Balkh*, a portrait of life in Ghazna. He then moved to Sarakhs, where he composed the *Seyr ol-'Ebâd ilâ 'l-Ma'âd*, dedicated to a religious authority in that city. Finally, he returned to Ghazna, which was under the rule of the Ghaznavid Bahrâm Shâh, to whom he dedicated some *qaside* and his principal work, the long didactic poem *Hadiqat ol-Haqiqe o Shari'at ot-Tariqe*. His life is generally divided into two distinct periods: initially he cultivated earthly and courtly interests, but subsequently devoted himself entirely to spiritual thinking. He is considered to be the first important mystical poet, who also laid the technical foundations for the ghazal. He wrote the earliest Sufi didactic *masnavi*. His works abound so much in religious references that they require commentaries and explanations. He was praised by the two later great mystical poets, 'Attâr and Rumi. His compositions include satirical and obscene lines often expressed in scurrilous language but at times also rhetorically refined, addressed to various types of people, even his own relatives. They mainly consists of *qet'e* (around a third of them), but similar lines are also found in the *Hadiqat ol-Haqiqe*. This production was met with very varied responses from the critics. According to some, influenced by the poet's spiritual tendencies, these lines should not be attributed to Sanâ'i, while others, anxious to circumscribe them, claim that they are lines only written during his time at court. It appears, on the contrary, that Sanâ'i wrote this kind of poetry throughout his life. He was the butt of satirical and obscene compositions by Suzani, one of the masters of the genre. The textual questions concerning his divan are particularly convoluted. He died in around 1130.

Shahid Originally from Balkh, he was active in the 10th century at the court of the Samanids, for whom he wrote *qaside*. An expert on philosophy and a skilled calligrapher, he composed both in Arabic and Persian and was greatly admired by other poets, such as his contemporaries Daqiqi and Rudaki (he wrote Shahid's funeral elegy), and later Farrokhi, Khâqâni, Manuchehri and Mo'ezzi. Around a hundred of his lines, characterised by intense content and a straightforward style, have survived. Only a few are of satirical and obscene inspiration. His probable year of death is 936.

Shamsi 'l-A'raj He was born in Bukhara, where he was active in the reign of the Âl-e Borhân, towards the end of the 12th century. He was lame and had a jovial and generous disposition. Only a few of his lines have survived.

Sharaf od-Din Yahyâ al-'Owfi He is the grandfather of the anthologist Moḥammad 'Owfi, the famous author of *Lobâb ol-Albâb*, who was probably born in around 1180. Thus he is likely to have flourished in the mid or late 12th century.

Shatranji Very probably originally from Samarkand, he was active in the 12th century in the service of the Qarakhanid sovereigns. Some sources claim that he was a student of the great satirical poet Suzani. Many of his surviving lines (a total of around a hundred, mostly *qet'e*) are effectively of the satirical type. He was highly skilled in using rhyme and complex refrains.

Suzani A great satirical poet, he was renowned for his crude obscene language. Born in Nasaf, near Samarkand, in around 1096, he spent most of his life in that city. He followed in his father's footsteps as a poet. His pen-name, Suzani, is derived from the word *suzan* ('needle') and he chose it, according to some sources, because of business matters or a love story involving a young tailor, but a more likely explanation is the sharp nature of his verse. He addressed most of his *qaside* to the Qarakhanid rulers of Samarkand, but he also praised the Bukhara religious authorities and the Saljuq sultan Sanjar. He is famed above all for his many satirical and obscene poems, which exercised a great influence over later authors. His texts on the penis, for example, inspired similar compositions by Pur-e Bahâ, and his parodies of Sanâ'i were among the sources of inspiration for various verse reworkings by 'Obeyd. Besides Sanâ'i, his illustrious 'victims' included Mo'ezzi, Nezâmi-ye 'Aruzi and Vatvât. His favourite target, however, was a poet whom he called Khar-e Khomkhâne ('Tavern Donkey'), the addressee of around a third of his satirical compositions.

His refrains on the pudenda are well known, as are some introductory obscene sections to his *qaside*. Among his models were the Arab poet Abu Nuwâs and the celebrated Anvari. In his verse he mentions, as illustrious predecessors, ʿAmʿaq, Hakkâk, Khatiri, Monjik, Qariʿ od-Dahr and Tayyân, while Shatranji was one of his followers. Suzani's satirical verse has great inventive power and is rich in rare and dialect terms. As such, it is also very interesting from the lexical point of view. At times his texts are difficult to interpret, and the difficulties are further complicated by the shortcomings of the current edition. He was one of the few authors to compose ghazals on satirical and obscene themes. According to some sources, late in life he was said to have expressed regrets about his obscene writings, but this suggestion may simply be a literary *topos*. He probably died in 1173/4.

Tayyân He was born near Marv and was active in the 10th century. Most of his around 80 surviving lines are playful and often use scurrilous language, hence his nickname Zhâzhkhây ('Fribble' or 'Chatterbox'). According to some sources, in old age he reneged on this behaviour and gave up poetry to became a stonemason. Suzani, the great master of satirical and obscene poetry, cites him as a predecessor. He is also mentioned by Anvari and Khâqâni.

Vatvât He was born in Balkh, probably in 1088/9. His real name was Mohammad and his title was Rashid od-Din. He is mainly known as Vatvât ('Bat'), a nickname due to his small height and baldness, which may have accounted for his bad-tempered nature. He was chief secretary of the Khwarazmshah ruler Atsiz, in whose honour he wrote several *qaside*. His poems are often refined from the formal point of view but the same cannot always be said for their content. His surviving texts include not only a good deal of poetry, but also an important work on rhetoric, entitled *Hadâʾeq os-Sehr fi Daqâʾeq osh-Sheʿr*, and numerous public and private letters, some in Persian and others in Arabic. He was initially a friend of two other poets, Adib Sâber and Khâqâni, but their relations deteriorated and he engaged in some fierce invective exchanges with them. He also had problematic relations with other poets, but few of his satirical and obscene lines have survived. Some considered him to be one of the most erudite men of his age. A possible date for is death 1182/3.

Zahir od-Din-e Fâryâbi As his name suggests he was born in Fâryâb, near Balkh, probably in around 1156. He wandered between various courts, but his most important patrons were the two Ildeguzid sovereigns of

Azerbaijan, Qezel Arslân and Abu Bakr, to whom he dedicated various *qaside*. He became famous as a panegyrist, but also wrote ghazals. He was an erudite poet, well versed in Arabic and several fields of knowledge. He wrote in a straightforward fluent style. He wrote only a few satirical and obscene lines. At the end of his life he left court circles and chose to lead a solitary existence. He died at Tabriz in 1201.

Glossary of Key Literary Terms

Chistân — Also known as *loghaz*, this kind of composition, a sort of riddle, is constructed as a series of questions inviting the reader to find a 'hidden' subject.

Fakhr — Literally 'self-praise', this term stands for poetry praising self.

Ghazal — The typical form of Persian lyrical poetry, used to express both earthly passion and mystical elation. Every line is rhymed, as is the end of the first hemistich of the initial line. Its length normally varies from five to fifteen lines. In the last line the poet usually includes his penname.

Habsiyyât — Poems composed in prison.

Hajv — This term is usually translated as 'satire', 'mockery', 'verbal aggression'.

Hazl — This term is usually translated as 'witticism', 'facetiae', 'bawdy poetry'.

Hejâ — See *hajv*.

Jedd — 'Earnestness' as opposed to *hazl*.

Madh/madih — Both *madh* and *madih* (more rarely *medhat*) are used to indicate panegyrical poetry: see *qaside*.

Mahju — The addressee of a *hajv* composition.

Marsiyye — An elegiac poem written in memory of a dead person.

Masnavi — A poetic form used for long compositions (epics, romances, didactic and religious poems, satires, etc.) that may even amount to tens of thousands of lines. The rhyme scheme is a kind of 'rhyming couplet', whereby the two hemistichs of each line are rhymed and the rhyme must be repeated as seldom as possible in nearby lines.

Mosammat — A poetic form made up of strophes with rhyming hemistichs, except for the last hemistich of each strophe, which has a different rhyme. The same rhyme is repeated in the last hemistich of each strophe, thus giving the overall composition a certain formal unity.

Nasib — See *qaside*.

Qaside — The principal form of panegyrical poetry, also used to express other content (philosophical, religious, didactic, elegiac, satirical, etc.). The classic scheme has two principal parts: a lyrical introduction (*nasib/tashbib*) on the themes of love, wine and Spring, and the panegyric (*madh/madih*). The two parts are linked by some transitional lines (*gorizgâh/takhallos*). The ends of each line rhyme, as does the end of the first hemistich in the initial line. The length of this form can vary from a few dozen to a few hundred lines.

Qetʿe — A poetic form often used to describe more unusual and less canonical themes, such as personal stories and affairs. It is the favoured vehicle for satirical and obscene poetry. Each line has an end rhyme and sometimes the rhyme is also present at the end of the first hemistich in the initial line. Its length can vary from a few lines to a few dozen lines.

Rendi — The typical attitude of the *rend*, a term variously translated as 'rake, libertine, lout or debauchee', which indicates a character antithetical to the deceitfulness and hypocrisy of the political, religious and social establishment. *Rendi* poetry is thus poetry of criticism and protest, highlighting values such as honesty, sincerity and true faith, also by resorting to outrageous and unorthodox symbols.

Robâʿi — A poetic form made up of two lines and, therefore, four hemistichs; hence the name *robâʿi* (quatrain). The classic scheme has rhymes at the end of the first, second and fourth hemistichs. Given its brevity, the *robâʿi* is mainly epigrammatic and used to express various kinds of content (philosophical, religious, gnomic, satirical, etc.).

Sahl-e momtaneʿ — Literally 'inimitable facility', this term indicates a poet's capacity to write in a perfect simple style that no one else is capable of emulating.

Shahrâshub	Literally meaning 'upsetting the town', this term indicates the poetic genre focused on the description of young craftsmen and servants whose beauty causes havoc in the town.
Tarji'band	A poetic form made up of strophes separated by the same line with the two hemistichs rhymed. In the strophes the rhyme can be at the end of each line or at the end of each hemistich. Each strophe usually has a different rhyme.
Tarkibband	A poetic form made up of strophes separated by a line that is different each time and has rhymed hemistichs. In the strophes the rhyme can be at the end of each line or at the end of each hemistich. Each strophe usually has a different rhyme.
Tazkere	An anthology devoted to poets and illustrious people providing biographical information and, in the case of poets, examples of their verse. There are two main types: general anthologies analysing the works of poets and other important people from the origins up to the period of the author of the *tazkere*; and specific anthologies devoted to particular themes, periods or groups of people. They may be divided either chronologically or geographically.
Tazmin	The quoting of hemistichs or lines by other, usually celebrated poets.
Zohd	Meaning 'abstinence', this term may also be used to indicate poetry on the theme of detachment from the earthly world.

Notes

Introduction

1 The two terms are both present in the poems presented in this book. *Hajv* is more often used in Persian studies and we have thus adopted this term in our comments and analyses.

2 For a survey of *hajv* and *hazl* in Classical Arabic literature see van Gelder 1988; van Gelder 1992. There are also those who argue that Persian *hajv* and *hazl* are completely independent of the Arabic models (Nikubakht 2001: 51–54).

3 Excursuses on *hajv* and *hazl* in Persian literature may be found in Behzâdi Anduhjerdi 1999; Behzâdi Anduhjerdi 2004, with a rich anthology; Dorri 1965: 5–16; Föllmer 2008; Halabi 1980: 1–138, up to the age of 'Obeyd (14th century); Halabi 1985; Halabi 1998; Javadi 1988; Kâseb 1991, with an excellent anthology; Kavir 1997; Mahjub 1967: 84–87, 470–474, 636, for only the Khorasanian style (11th century); Mo'tamen 1967: 307–330; Nikubakht 2001, with a comprehensive classification and a good anthology; Rastegâr-e Fasâyi 1993: 227–258; Safâ 1954: II: 354–356; III: 86–97, 323; V: 628–631; Salâhi 2003; Sprachman 1981: 67–88, up to the age of 'Obeyd; Sprachman 1988; Sprachman 1995. For some recent articles on *hajv* and *hazl* of the period dealt with here see Zipoli 1994; Zipoli 1995; Zipoli 1996; Zipoli 1997; Zipoli 2001; Zipoli 2002; Zipoli 2006; Zipoli 2008; Zipoli 2010; see also Zipoli 2011; Zipoli 2015. Interesting remarks about the social background of some of our anecdotes can be found in Floor 2008.

4 In Persian texts both *madh* and *madih* (more rarely *medhat*) are used to indicate panegyric.

5 Key Kâ'us 1973: 190.

6 Hârun ar-Rashid was the fifth caliph (r. 786–809) of the Abbasid dynasty.

7 Beyhaqi 1945: 30. Ma'mun is one of Hârun ar-Rashid's sons involved in the power struggle for the caliphate.

8 Shams-e Qeys 1981: 459.

9 Nezâmi-ye ʻAruzi 1967: 75–83. The entire *hajv* is in Ferdowsi 1990: 98–106 (*dibâche*). Regarding the authenticity of this text see de Blois 1992: 119; Nazir Ahmad 1991: 1–20.

10 Ferdowsi 1990: 105 (*dibâche*).

11 Shams-e Qeys 1981: 454.

12 Rumi 1925: I: 113.

13 ʻOwfi 1903: II: 203–204.

14 Anvari 1959: 330.

15 Kamâl od-Din 1970: 675.

16 Asadi 1977: 160.

17 Key Kâʼus 1973: 191.

18 Jabali 1977: 15.

19 Khâqâni 1997: 1243.

20 See Anvari's retractions (Anvari 1959: 483), the fairly unlikely recanting of Suzani (d. c. 1174) recorded both in his poems (Suzani 1959: 250–251) and in other sources (Dowlatshâh 1987: 79; ʻOwfi 1903: II: 191), and the justifications which accompany the omission of similar passages (Dowlatshâh 1987: 79, 90, 218, 332). In modern times, this diffidence seems to have acquired stronger, though not more convincing, tones. Some of the usual reasons advanced by scholars to attenuate the impropriety of the poets, thus justifying them, are youthfulness, as in the case of Sanâʼi (d. c. 1130) (Sanâʼi 1983: *shast o yek*); encroaching senility, as in the case of Rumi (Rumi 1925: VI: VII); humble origins, as in the cases of Anvari, Suzani and Khâqâni (Shebli Noʻmâni 1984: IV: 129–130); and, in general, the corrupt times (Moʼtamen 1967: 318, 327–328; Safâ 1954: II: 356). Not infrequently this 'deviant' behaviour is said to have originated in the dominant Arabic models which the Persians would have simply emulated (Moʼtamen 1967: 307; Safâ 1954: II: 354). For further references on this issue see Zipoli 1994: 257–259.

21 Key Kâʼus 1973: 191.

22 Manuchehri 1977: 139.

23 Jamâl od-Din 1941: 265.

24 Bertel's 1988: 400. Bertel's' account is also important, and convincing, in its rejection of a realistic tendency in *hajv* poetry. We share his view, and believe that what we have said on the subject of anti-realistic obscenity in Persian poetry (Zipoli 1994: 262–265) can be extended to the production of *hajv*. At the same time, however, it cannot be denied that this kind of poetry does give glimpses of some typical situations and mechanisms in the society of the time.

25 Râduyâni 1949: 47. Not only pen-names, but also evocative nicknames are used, such as Kun-e Mardom ('People's Arse') in the case of Ruhi (12th century) ('Owfi 1903: II: 165).

26 Askari n.d.: 148.

27 Beyhaqi 1945: 468.

28 Manuchehri 1977: 72–73.

29 The *adab* literature consists of texts aimed at conveying those forms of general knowledge which in the Islamic world are indispensable for a cultivated man to play an active part in social life. To make the often difficult texts more attractive to read, the authors sometimes add playful and even obscene anecdotes.

30 See, for example, Javadi 1988: 13–14, 16; Mo'tamen 1967: 307.

31 Nâser-e Khosrow 1956: 532.

32 With the more irreverent *hazl*, like the similar *hajv* (see note 20), disavowals and justifications of a conventional kind are frequent in various authors' work; see the implausible declarations made by Khâqâni (Khâqâni 1997: 796, 1181), the suspect pleading by Sa'di (d. 1292) (Sa'di 1995: 989) and the last-minute second thoughts in Râvandi's *Râhat os-Sodur o Âyat os-Sorur* (completed c. 1204) (Râvandi 1921: 457–458). The prudish reasons advanced in some cases for omitting the passages in question are significant in this context ('Owfi 1903: II: 175, 198).

33 Asadi 1940: 49.

34 Sanâ'i 1989: 686.

35 Rumi 1925: III: 8.

36 Owhadi 1996: 586.

37 'Attâr 2007: 153.

38 Nasrollâh Monshi 1964: 18. These interpretations follow some specific lines of *adab* literature: see note 29.

39 Anvari 1959: 398.

40 Sanâ'i 1981: 202.

41 'Obeyd 1999: 257.

42 Jâmi 1999b: I: 670–671.

43 Sanâ'i 1989: 718.

44 Rumi 1925: V: 160.

45 Rumi 1925: IV: 489.

46 Sa'di 1995: 89.

47 'Obeyd 1999: 324.

48 Key Kâ'us 1973: 78.

49 Key Kâ'us 1973: 204–205.

50 Nezâm ol-Molk 1962: 113–114, 154.
51 Shams-e Qeys 1981: 459–460.
52 We have followed the text in Meier 1963: 9; see also van Gelder 1995: 125; Halabi 1980: 81; Kâseb 1991: 43–45; Qazvini 1953: I, 39–42. On this episode and the earliest examples of satirical poetry in Persian see also Nikubakht 2001: 216–220; Safâ 1954: I, 148–149.
53 Some Persian authors of *hajv* and *hazl* directly allude to their Arab predecessors, such as Suzani who refers to Abu Nuwâs, the famous Arab poet who wrote some celebrated texts on erotic and Bacchic themes (Suzani 1959: 59). Abu Nuwâs was born at Ahvâz in 756, of a Persian mother and Arab father; he died in Baghdad in 814.
54 See Dorri 1965: 5–6; Kâseb 1991: 46; Qazvini 1953: I: 43–45.
55 The presence of *hajv* and *hazl* in Persian popular ballads has been documented by Zhukovskiĭ 1902: 4.
56 Bertel's 1960: 127.
57 This trend is described and documented in Zipoli 1996: 279–280. Significantly, in this context, the Steingass *Persian-English Dictionary* very often includes obscene interpretations of its lemmas (Zipoli 2011).
58 For Ferdowsi's *hajv* see note 9.
59 The poem is translated below (see the text with note 183).
60 The texts of this dispute are in Hedâyat 1957: I: 922–929; for an analysis of these poems see Zarrinkub 1982: 191–195.
61 For the spread of *hajv/hazl* in the Timurid period see Dowlatshâh 1987; Navâ'i 1984. For some quotations see Yârshâter 1955: 234–238.
62 For reasons of space we could not include in our corpus the whole of any of the *masnavi* of interest from the *hajv/hazl* point of view. We only quote examples from Sanâ'i's *Kârnâme-ye Balkh* (see the text with note 228) and from the *masnavi* on the courtesans of the Ghaznavid prince Shirzâd (ruler in the year 1115) by Mas'ud-e Sa'd (d. c. 1122) (see the text with note 230). Other significant *masnavi* include that on the judge Tâj od-Din Amzâd (known as *Hajv-e Qâzi-ye Kirang*) by Anvari (Anvari 1959: 477–483); that on Shehâb od-Din 'Omar-e Lonbâni by Kamâl od-Din (Kamâl od-Din 1970: 450–456); and the *Kârnâme-ye Owqâf*, traditionally associated with a certain Tâj od-Din-e Nesâ'i (Nesâ'i 1960: 5–22) but recently attributed to Pur-e Bahâ (d. c. 1284) (Hoffmann 1990). For useful information on the satirical *masnavi* described as *kârnâme* see Nikubakht 2001: 126–130.
63 Namely, a *tarji'band* by 'Obeyd translated below (see the text with note 351) and its antecedent by Jamâl od-Din-e Kâshi, a 13th-century Ilkhanid poet, on whom little information has come down to us (Mohammad ebn-e

Badr-e Jâjarmi 1959: 919–924). On these two works see Sprachman 1981: 109–118; Zipoli 1994. For some ghazals with *hajv* contents see Skalmowski 1999: 83–95.

64 For recent Persian examples of this attitude see Akhavân Sâles 1995: 37–39, 79, 116–118; Nikubakht 2001: 103, 256, 285, 287, 307, 322. Some comments on this are in Zipoli 1994: 255–257.

65 Bausani was one of the first to complain about the lack of research on this 'particularly interesting' field of Persian obscene poetry which 'for false reasons of prudery has never been studied accurately' (Bausani 1960: 422). Another more recent appeal for further research can be found in Halabi 1998: 11–12. This kind of backwardness ia also present in the area of Persian humorous prose works (Marzolph 1992: I, 13–14, 21). Moreover, it is important to bear in mind that the few references in the various literary histories are all very superficial and usually contain negative judgements. In this context, Sprachman's meagre excursus is significant (Sprachman 1988), although elsewhere he has dealt with the subject at greater length (Sprachman 1981; Sprachman 1995). Some useful studies have been published in Iran: Halabi 1985; Kâseb 1991; Halabi 1998; Nikubakht 2001; Shamisâ 2002.

66 The ancient Roman poet Martial, active in the 1st century, is mainly known for his epigrams containing acute, trenchant and also obscene satires. Another ancient Roman poet, Juvenal, who lived in the late 1st and early 2nd centuries, was famed for his often scurrilous satires on contemporary society. In Latin studies there is even a tendency to identify the whole output of an author like Horace only with his satires.

67 Zarrinkub 1992: 168.

68 At times the attributions are controversial. The confused textual tradition is made more uncertain in some cases by the fact that the poets would attribute their own *hajv/hazl* to rivals, thus bringing them into disrepute.

69 The division of the poets into a chronology required a conventional choice when the author was active over two centuries. In these cases the reference point adopted was the date of death of the poet (who therefore is situated in the second of the two centuries in question), unless he lived and flourished mainly in the first of the two centuries (which thus becomes the relevant temporal reference). The situation is particularly uncertain in the earliest two centuries (10th and 11th) due to the lack of precise biographical information. Within each century, the poets are listed in alphabetical order.

70 The *tazkere* are anthologies devoted to poets and illustrious figures containing biographical information and, in the case of poets, accompanied by some examples of their verse.

71 We have followed the technique proposed by Highet in studying satire: 'One of the best ways to study the problem of form in literature is the method used by Aristotle. This is induction. First, collect as many examples of a given phenomenon as possible. Then, by observing resemblances and differences and contrasts and alliances, extract from these particulars a few general descriptive principles' (Highet 1962: 13). In addition to Highet's book, other works particularly useful in defining our corpus have been Griffin 1994; Hodgart 1969; Test 1991.

72 Obviously the *mahju* may not be the same person as the poet's interlocutor as when, for example, the author turns to someone to criticise someone else.

73 Except for *masnavi* (see note 62) and a few other cases (see the texts with notes 157, 212 and 348), we have always translated whole compositions. At times, therefore, we quote lines not strictly within the *hajv/hazl* theme, but this serves the purpose of giving a general idea of the contexts that the passages belong to. Translating was sometimes problematic both because of the intrinsic difficulties of this kind of poetry and because of the lack of good editions. In addition, some of the more risqué parts have been 'suppressed' by the editors (Zipoli 1994: 255–256). This obliged us to various delicate salvage operations.

74 In this kind of poetry, the gap between the original texts and translations is wider than in serious poetry. In fact, as mentioned above, accurately interpreting *hajv/hazl* compositions is a complex operation and implies a knowledge both of the traditional models and their violations: it is a kind of twofold code. Paradoxically, the function and importance of form in these texts are given greater emphasis, precisely because of their outrageous content which, on the other hand, in translation may lead unwitting readers to believe they are dealing with only primitive and crude compositions.

Chapter 1 – Invective Poetry

75 Asadi 1977: 92.

76 Asadi 1977: 89.

77 Asadi 1977: 21.

78 Sanâ'i 1983: 1105.

79 A line attributed to Bu 'l-Horr is in Asadi 1940: 455.

80 Asadi 1977: 56.

81 Asadi 1977: 126.
82 Asadi 1977: 30.
83 Asadi 1977: 92.
84 Sâm Mirzâ n.d.: 209. Nimrod, the king of Babylon who refused to convert to monotheism, is a symbol of pagan perversion.
85 Asadi 1977: 176.
86 Asadi 1977: 146.
87 Anvari 1959: 461.
88 Khâju 1957: 164.
89 Asadi 1977: 15.
90 Asadi 1977: 167.
91 Asadi 1940: 76.
92 Asadi 1977: 163.
93 Asadi 1977: 139.
94 Asadi 1977: 25.
95 Asadi 1940: 254, first line; 82, second line.
96 Qomri 1989: 589.
97 Qomri 1989: 619.
98 Musk is a sweet-smelling black substance produced by the navel of the musk deer.
99 Asadi 1977: 26.
100 Asadi 1977: 153.
101 Asadi 1977: 128.
102 Asadi 1977: 23.
103 Asadi 1977: 113. A recurrent topos in this kind of poetry (Zipoli 1995: 209), the artificial penis obviously alludes to passive sexuality.
104 Asadi 1977: 76.
105 Asir od-Din 1958: 420.
106 In this world the absence of hair on the female pubes is considered to be attractive.
107 Edârechi Gilâni 1991: 310; the second line is also in Asadi 1977: 176.
108 'Owfi 1903: II: 202.
109 Sanâ'i 1983: 1098–1099.
110 Asadi 1977: 81.
111 Homâm 1972: 208.
112 Anvari 1959: 432.
113 Asadi 1977: 26.
114 Guzgânân is the name of a region in eastern Khorasan, between Balkh and Marv.

115 Sanâ'i 1983: 1075.
116 Âzar 1957: 1198.
117 Asadi 1940: 147.
118 This may be Abu 'l-'Abbâs al-Fazl ebn-e 'Abbâs al-Rabenjâni: see de Blois 1992: 61.
119 Âzar 1958: 338.
120 Sanâ'i 1983: 1051–1052. The last hemistich is also used by Sanâ'i in another poem (see the text with note 278).
121 Meier 1963: 264. The onset of the beard is the cause and also symbol of the decline of the beauty of the young beloved.
122 Qomri 1989: 554.
123 'Ârefak's title is actually Serâj od-Din, 'Lantern of faith': see 'Owfi 1903: II: 385.
124 'Owfi 1903: II: 385.
125 Shalfiyye is synonymous of a woman of loose morals. A female character with this name is the protagonist in a lascivious story entitled *Alfiyye o Shalfiyye*, believed to have been composed on the basis of pre-Islamic traditions of Indian origins by the 11th-century poet Azraqi. Some scholars claim that this poem, which has not come down to us, was accompanied by images and was written to cure the impotence of the prince Toghân Shâh, Azraqi's patron: see de Blois 1992: 92–93.
126 'Owfi 1903: II: 208.
127 The allusion is to the small size of the member of the person being insulted.
128 Suzani is mentioned here as a famous author of poems on the male member.
129 Qamar 1984: 200.
130 Lâme'i 1976: 20.
131 Lâme'i 1976: 114.
132 Ghur, a region in Afghanistan, was considered to be a land of infidels. Moreover, *ghur* also means a depraved, effeminate man, thus alluding to a possible offence which creates an even more disparaging picture. In addition to being the cradle of unbelievers, India was famous for providing the Persian courts with pages and slaves.
133 The term 'Antichrist' is the translation of Dajjâl. In the Islamic eschatological tradition, he was a monstrous malevolent character who, according to some sources, will make a brief appearance at the end of time, riding on a donkey, it too monstrous, and encouraging, among other things, adultery and sodomy.
134 'Am'aq n.d.: 173–176.

Chapter 2 – Satirical Poetry

135 ʿOwfi 1903: II: 240.
136 Sanâ'i 1983: 1094.
137 Anvari 1959: 366.
138 Zahir od-Din 1982: 306b.
139 Kamâl od-Din 1970: 440.
140 Anvari 1959: 330.
141 Zahir od-Din 1982: 297–298.
142 Sanâ'i 1983: 1087–1088.
143 Sanâ'i 1983: 1075.
144 ʿOwfi 1903: II: 4.
145 Enju 1980: 2034–2035.
146 ʿOwfi 1903: II: 297.
147 Salmân n.d.: 430. The last hemistich is a Persian proverb, meaning 'there can be nothing worse'. This poem represents a minor category of satire involving horses; for other examples see Anvari 1959: 135; Kamâl od-Din 1970: 442; ʿOwfi 1903: II: 114–117.
148 Kamâl od-Din 1970: 681.
149 Kamâl od-Din 1970: 621.
150 The seven members are the two hands, the two feet, the head, the chest and the back.
151 The Islamic tradition recognises eight different levels of paradise and nine celestial spheres (the seven planets plus the sphere of fixed stars and the sphere moving all the others).
152 Mojir od-Din 1979: 321–322.
153 For Abu Nuwâs see note 53.
154 Rostam is a famous hero in the Iranic epopee and the most important character in Ferdowsi's *Shâhnâme*. He was a central figure in the struggle between Iran (the civilised world) and Turân (the land of barbarians and the steppe).
155 Sâm and Narimân are two legendary heroes whose deeds are narrated in Ferdowsi's *Shâhnâme*. They are respectively the grandfather and great grandfather of Rostam (see the previous note).
156 This is a twofold affront: the poet not only denies his favours but also acts offensively. He says he is unable to satisfy the patron's erotic requests, blaming the patron himself for having abused the poet's favours in the past, thus undermining his sexual prowess.
157 ʿOwfi 1903: II: 169–170.

158 'Owfi 1903: II: 297.
159 Khâju 1957: 161.
160 Bâvard, better known as Abivard, is the name of a city in northern Khorasan.
161 Dowlatshâh 1987: 318.
162 Nezâri 1992: 131–132. According to a method typical of Persian poetry, at times the poet addresses himself using, as in this case, the third person or, as in other poems, the second person (see note 165).
163 For musk see note 98.
164 According to tradition, Solomon, the renowned king and prophet, possessed a ring that gave him magical powers. As a punishment for his misbelief, the ring was stolen by a *jinn* (a supernatural being, half man and half angel) who, for a certain period, ruled in Solomon's place.
165 In Persian poetry, sometimes the poet addresses himself using the second person (see note 162).
166 Farghâni 1985: 118–120.
167 In the Persian lyrical-mystical literature, the Old Man of the Magi is an esoteric and spiritual master who introduces disciples to the mysteries of life. The Magi are described in Persian poetry as the ritual representatives, associated with fire and wine, of the religion founded by Zarathustra.
168 Hâfez 1983: 406. The Persian term translated as 'cleric' is *Hâfez*. It literally means 'one who knows the Koran by heart' and is also the pen-name of the poet, which is usually found at the end of a ghazal. The *mufti* is an expert in Islamic law authorised to pronounce juridical-religious sentences.
169 Bohlul (d. c. 805) is the archetipe of the 'wise fool' genre in Arabic and Persian literature. For Hârun see note 6.
170 'Attâr 2007: 117.
171 Nezâmi-ye 'Aruzi 1967: 74.
172 Farrokhi (d. 1037) and 'Onsori (d. 1039) were two celebrated panegyrists at the Ghaznavid court and the first major exponents of the early style of Persian poetry known as the Khorasanian style.
173 Râduyâni 1949: 32. On these lines see de Blois 1992: 180–181.
174 A contemporary of Jâmi and his rival, Sâghari was a 15th-century poet notorious for his poor verse-making.
175 Jâmi 1999a: I: 841.
176 Râmtin was a celebrated Sassanid-age musician thought to have invented the harp; he was probably active during the reign of Khosrow Parviz (590–628).
177 For musk see note 98.

178 According to Islamic doctrine, the houris are virgins awaiting the devout in paradise.
179 These pairs of letters from the Arabo-Persian alphabet are distinguished only by the presence of some dots.
180 Ray was once in the territories of the Ghaznavid dynasty, at whose court Manuchehri was a poet.
181 Shervân, a region of the eastern Caucasus, was ruled by the Shirvanshah dynasty from the 11th to the early 16th centuries.
182 Moʿtasem and Mostaʿin were two caliphs in the Abbasid dynasty. The first ruled from 833 to 842, the second from 862 to 866.
183 Manuchehri 1977: 79–82.
184 A 'tavern' would literally be 'where they store vats of wine'. For this poet see de Blois 1994: 341–342.
185 Since Kash was in Transoxiana, the expression 'from Kash to Kashmir' means a vast geographical expanse.
186 In the Islamic tradition, Mercury is said to offer protection to and encourage men of science.
187 Zâl and Hojir are two epic heroes whose deeds are narrated in Ferdowsi's *Shâhnâme*. Zâl is the father of the great Rostam (see note 154) and Hojir is the custodian of the famous White Fort.
188 Suzani 1959: 43–45.
189 See de Blois 1994: 548. There are also different opinions: see Nikubakht 2001: 135, 272.
190 The Samanids dynasty was of Persian origin and ruled from 819 to 999 in Transoxiana and in a large part of Iran.
191 Mazdikat is the name of a town near Samarkand.
192 Suzani 1959: 62–64.
193 For Ghur see note 132.
194 Shavvâl is the tenth month of the Islamic lunar year.
195 Khâqâni 1997: 931–932; in lines 3 and 10 we have followed the variants in Khâqâni 1937: 650. On the character mentioned in the final hemistich see de Blois 1994: 339.
196 The Homâ is a mythical bird, whose shadow is a harbinger of protection and good fortune.
197 According to popular tradition, the snake entered the earthly paradise concealed in the peacock's beak. The sparrow is noted for its copious droppings.
198 Khâqâni 1997: 1225–1226.
199 Khâqâni, in turn, makes *hajv* on Abu 'l-ʿAlâ' (Khâqâni 1978: 235–237); on

the relations between the two poets and their dispute in poetry: see de Blois 1994: 247–249.

200 Âzar 1957: 205.

201 Shervân is the Caucasian region in which Khâqâni was born: see note 181.

202 Amin Ahmad n.d.: III: 299–300; on the last line see de Blois 1994: 248.

203 Alexander, the Macedonian king and conqueror of the ancient Persian empire, is a character adopted by the Islamic-Persian tradition. As such, he is seen not as a foreign enemy but as a hero with prophetic aspects. In poetry he is mentioned, among other things, for his vain search for the water of life and for the mirror, which he ordered to be placed on the tower of Alexandria so that he could look out for enemy ships. His legendary deeds inspired many Persian poems, the most famous being the *Eskandarnâme* by Nezâmi-ye Ganjavi. Here the poet wishes to stress that Khâqâni's soul was so black that it could not be 'brightened', even if Alexander's skill transformed it into a mirror.

204 The Persian text plays on a pun of an astrological nature. In the Arabo-Persian tradition the two constellations of the Bear (Ursa Major and Ursa Minor) are both called Banât on-Na'sh ('The daughters of the coffin'): four stars form the coffin and three are the daughters. More precisely, Ursa Major is called Banât on-Na'sh-e Kabir and Ursa Minor Banât on-Na'sh-e Saghir. Here the allusion is to Ursa Minor, which includes the North or Pole Star, a universal reference point. Since the addressee of these lines boasts of being as essential as the Pole Star, Mojir od-Din replies that he is indeed like the pole, but only because no one is near him except the coffin of his daughter, thus alluding to Ursa Minor (the two terms, 'daughter' and 'coffin', are simply inverted) as well as to the abandonment and solitude that an unattended funeral evokes.

205 Khâqâni wrote *hajv* lines against his own father (see the text with note 281). Mojir od-Din might have insinuated here that he wrote them ('cutting off his nose to spite his face') in the hope of being compared to the carpenter's son, i.e. Abraham (mentioned in the following line), who also disowned his father, Âzar, but for noble reasons. Âzar was a famous idolator and builder of pagan wooden idols, hence Mojir od-Din's use of the epithet 'carpenter'.

206 Hedâyat 1957: I: 1188. The reference in the last hemistich is to the Koranic episode in which Nimrod threw Abraham onto a pyre, but Abraham came off unscathed because the Lord ordered that the fire 'be coolness and safety' (Koran 1955: XXI, 69). Hence the many allusions in Persian poetry to flames being transformed, through love and faith, into a rose garden. But the opposite applies to the addressee of these lines: a delicate, fragrant basil

plant is transformed into a tormenting fire. Hedâyat considered the lines translated here to be on Khâqâni, but they also appear in a long *qaside* addressed to Zeyn od-Din-e Tabari in Mojir od-Din's divan (Mojir od-Din 1979: *bist o do—bist o se*, 125–131; see Foruzânfar 1979: 588; Halabi 1998: 542–543). See also Khâqâni 1989: *chehel o hasht*.

207 For Shervân see note 201.

208 Emru 'l-Qeys was one of the leading Arab poets in the pre-Islamic period; he lived in the first half of the 6th century. Sahbân was a celebrated Arab orator and rhetorician who lived during the reign of the caliph Mu'âwiya (r. 661–680).

209 According to tradition, cumin was a typical product of Kerman, so this phrase is the equivalent of 'carrying coals to Newcastle'.

210 The ant is associated with Solomon in a Koranic story (Koran 1955: XXVII, 18–19): an ant complains to Solomon that his advancing army would crush his companions, and the powerful sovereign pays heed to it. This motif is used to represent the generosity of noble souls and the contrast between two incommensurable positions. The contrast is emphasised by the modest gift, a locust leg, which, according to one tradition, the ant gave to Solomon.

211 Tayyân was a 10th-century poet who also wrote playful and obscene poems; some are included in this anthology.

212 Jamâl od-Din 1941: 85–86. Hassân was an Arab author who lived in the 7th century; he was the official poet of the prophet Muhammad.

213 A satire on Isfahan by Mojir od-Din is quoted below (see the text with note 289). On the consequences of this satire for relations between Mojir od-Din, Jamâl od-Din and Khâqâni see Nikubakht 2001: 123–125; Zipoli 2002: 466–470.

214 Shervân and Beylaqân are the home towns of Khâqâni and Mojir od-Din respectively, both targets for Jamâl od-Din's satire.

215 Jamâl od-Din 1941: 400–401.

216 Jamâl od-Din 1941: 402.

217 Amin Ahmad n.d.: II: 87. The bridge in question is called Serât (it is wide for the virtuous and very narrow for sinners). According to the Islamic eschatology, the bridge crosses hell and leads to paradise.

218 Vatvât 1960: 570. The city of Basra was renowned for the superior quality of its dates.

219 In this and the following lines, the poet alludes to events involving Khosrow, Shirin and Farhâd. Khosrow was a famous Sassanid sovereign who ruled from 590 to 628 and Shirin was an Armenian princess. Their love

story and the feud between Khosrow and Farhâd, a rival to the Sassanid sovereign in his love for Shirin, are the subject of many Persian poems; the most celebrated is *Khosrow o Shirin* by Nezâmi-ye Ganjavi.

220 The poet left his native town of Ardabil and spent some time in the region of Shervân, at the Shirvanshah court in the Caucasus, where he began to write the *Farhâdnâme*.

221 In Persian poetry allusion is often made to the great skills, as a painter, of Mâni, the prophet and founder of Manichaeism.

222 ʿÂref 1976: 137–139.

223 *Tâbe* and *âftâbe* mean 'pan' and 'water-pot', respectively.

224 The meanings of the four words are: 'bowl' and 'book', 'cup' and 'grief'.

225 For Mercury see note 186.

226 Sanâ'i 1989: 647–648.

227 Sanâ'i 1989: 697.

228 Sanâ'i 1981: 202–203.

229 Suzani 1959: 450.

230 Masʿud-e Saʿd 1939: 571–572.

231 Qomri 1989: 528.

232 Meier 1963: 266.

233 Meier 1963: 169. The last two comments seem to reproach the butcher for being overly zealous in his work and consequently neglecting his lovers. But it may also be an allusion to his insatiable sexual desire.

234 For Zuzan see Meier 1963: 308.

235 Meier 1963: 308.

236 Meier 1963: 184. Regarding the onset of the beard see note 121.

237 This is the hood covering the head of the falcon when it is ready to hunt.

238 This piece of poetry has been taken from ʿAttâr's *Manteq ot-Teyr*, which narrates how the hoopoe invites some other birds to go to the mythical bird called Simorgh.

239 ʿAttâr 1963: 53–54.

240 For the *mufti* see note 168.

241 Khayyâm 1959: II: 27 Persian numeration.

242 The *menbar* is a kind of pulpit in the mosque. The *mehrâb* is a niche in the mosque that indicates the *qibla*, i.e. the direction of Mecca, and to which the faithful turn when saying prayers.

243 For the Old Man of the Tavern/of the Magi see note 167.

244 Hâfez 1983: 404.

245 Hâfez 1983: 774.

246 Khayyâm 1931: 203.

247 Sa'di 1995: 995. Muslim prayers, recited standing and kneeling, are led by an imam, who faces Mecca with his back to the congregation.
248 For the *mehrâb* see note 242.
249 Sanâ'i 1989: 668–670. On the attitude of the Sufis towards love for young boys see Shamisâ 2002: 95–141.
250 Leaning the forehead on the prayer rug is one of the ritual positions during Muslim prayers.
251 Qomri 1989: 557.
252 For musk see note 98.
253 Sa'di 1995: 1000–1001. Sprachman points out that many of the lines in this poem were used in *Loghatnâme-ye Dehkhodâ* as examples in numerous entries (Sprachman 1995: XXXV, 39). This corroborates a consolidated Persian lexicographic tradition which involves searching for and using obscene sources. For this lexicographic tradition see note 57.
254 Joseph is a recurrent character in Persian poetry. He features in Sura XII of the Koran, in which his parable is described as 'the fairest of stories' (Koran 1955: XII, 3). Jacob's favourite son, he made his brothers jealous because they envied his good luck. They threw him in a well and told their father he had been devoured by a wolf. Joseph was renowned for his handsomeness, which is celebrated in many texts.
255 Owhadi 1996: 564–566.
256 A *tafsir* is a commentary of the Koran and a *hadith* is an account of a saying or deed of the prophet Muhammad.
257 Koran 1955: XLIX, 12.
258 Jâmi 1999b: I: 189–193.
259 In the following lines some questions are asked whether formulas and rituals typical of the pilgrimage to Mecca have been properly performed.
260 The reference is to Sura XVIII of the Koran, describing how seven young believers took refuge in a cave to flee from the paganism of their own people.
261 Nâser-e Khosrow 1986: 300–301.
262 Nâser-e Khosrow 1956: 505.
263 Khayyâm 1959: II: 58 Persian numeration.
264 Nezâmi-ye Ganjavi 1954: 144.
265 Anvari 1959: 441.
266 Asadi 1977: 88.
267 Asadi 1977: 140.
268 'Owfi 1903: II: 206.
269 Asadi 1977: 22.

270 The shapes of *jim* and *mim*, two letters in the Arabo-Persian alphabet, recall the curve of a curl and a rounded open mouth, respectively.
271 Mohammad ebn-e Badr-e Jâjarmi 1959: 1214. The author of these lines, Ebn-e Khatib, was involved in a famous love affair with Mahsati, characterised by exchanges of satirical and outrageous poems narrated in a text of uncertain date but 14th century: see Meier 2005.
272 Qamar 1984: 277.
273 Khâqâni 1997: 1070; in lines 9 and 10 we have followed the variants in Khâqâni 1937: 691.
274 Meier 1963: 370.
275 Suzani 1959: 479–480.
276 Sanâ'i 1989: 658–659.
277 Ebn-e Yamin 1965: 383.
278 Sanâ'i 1983: 1052.
279 For Âzar and Nimrod see notes 205 and 84, respectively. Joseph the carpenter is the husband of Mary, mother of Jesus.
280 For the *menbar* see note 242.
281 Khâqâni 1997: 1196–1197.
282 Anvari 1959: 358.
283 Anvari 1959: 401.
284 The Koran and the Bible relate how God, when exhorting Moses to pursue his mission as a prophet, showed him some miracles. Thus he told him to throw his stick on the ground, and it was immediately transformed into a snake (Bible 2011: Exodus 4, 2–4; Koran 1955: XX, 17–21).
285 Mas'ud-e Sa'd 1939: 611.
286 For some examples on other social categories or groups see the texts with notes 226, 227, 228, 229. On *shahrâshub* as a collective satirical composition see Nikubakht 2001: 120–126.
287 'Owfi 1903: II: 297.
288 Anvari 1959: 444.
289 Mojir od-Din 1979: 396. For this satire see note 213.
290 Khâqâni 1997: 1153.
291 Asir od-Din 1958: 441–442.
292 Anvari 1959: 401.
293 For another poem with the same addressee see the text with note 134.
294 For the Magi see note 167.
295 'Am'aq n.d.: 170–172.
296 The early-morning noise of a fart (the unpleasant surrogate for the fragrant breeze) makes the dawn despair. At the same time, the breaking up of the

sky's dress in the early morning is synonymous with dawn itself. Thus in an eccentric and disrespectful 'fantastic etiology', the fart seems to cause the day to break.

297 What we have translated as 'wet gherkin' is in Persian *gauz/guz-e tar*. This expression literally means 'fresh walnut' or 'wet fart'. We tried to recreate the wordplay with our pun on 'gurk' (a kind of fart) and 'gherkin'.

298 For musk see note 98.

299 The name of this town is not random: the word *guzdân* may literally also mean 'place containing farts'.

300 Here the tongue is sharper than the sword, which consequently takes issue with its own inadequate sharpness.

301 Kamâl od-Din 1970: 434–438.

302 The reference is to faeces that may be expelled at the moment of penetration.

303 This is an elaborate erotic gastronomic reference. Herbs were used to make yogurt tastier. The poet uses this image in a twofold humiliation of his victim: the herbs in the bowl are the hairs on the posterior, a repulsive image which, by resorting to an equally humiliating 'fantastic etiology', the poet associates with the *mahju*'s desire to taste the yogurt, in this case the sap from 'living' radishes.

304 Qomri 1989: 292–293.

305 Asadi 1940: 174.

306 Anvari 1959: 371.

307 Jamâl od-Din 1941: 428.

308 Asadi 1977: 15.

309 Khayyâm 1959: II: 52 Persian numeration.

310 Homâm 1972: 186.

311 Ebn-e Yamin 1965: 391.

312 Ebn-e Yamin 1965: 380–381.

313 'Owfi 1903: I: 178.

314 Sa'di 1995: 140–141.

315 'Attâr 1963: 120–121.

316 For Joseph see note 254.

317 Koran 1955: LII, 30.

318 Koran 1955: XLI, 17.

319 This is a reference to Sura LV of the Koran, dealing with the great mercifulness of the Creator.

320 Koran 1955: VII, 29.

321 Rumi 1925: V: 86–91.

322 The marriage portion that a husband must pay his wife if he divorces her for no good reason.

323 Sa'di 1995: 1001–1004. The wish in the last hemistich is from Koran 1955: II, 197; III, 14; III, 188.

324 Owhadi 1996: 549–550.

325 According to an ancient Zoroastrian custom, incestuous relations, especially in the noble classes, were not only allowed, they were even encouraged (Floor 2008: 2–3, 11). For the Magi see note 167.

326 Mokhtâri 1962: 222–226.

327 Mohammad ebn-e Badr-e Jâjarmi 1959: 871.

328 Mohammad ebn-e Badr-e Jâjarmi 1959: 871.

Chapter 3 – Burlesque Poetry

329 For Rostam see note 154.

330 'Obeyd 1999: 240–241.

331 On the parodic use of the exordium in Arabic and Persian poetry see Meisami 2003: 144–189.

332 This is a reference to Moses' reproach to his brother Aaron, narrated in the Bible (Bible 2011: Exodus 32, 21–22) and the Koran (Koran 1955: XX, 92–95); in the Koran there is a specific allusion to Moses grasping Aaron's beard.

333 This prince can probably be identified as the Shaddadid ruler Fazl III (1073–1075).

334 Hedâyat 1957: II: 648.

335 For Khosrow, Shirin and Farhâd (mentioned below) see note 219.

336 The belt and crown are characteristic of royalty and here allude to the shape of the male member after circumcision; in the following lines the poet goes on to conjure up the circumcision ceremony.

337 This is an allusion to the erect or relaxed position of the male member, which is supported—in a different way in the two cases—by the testicles and pubic hair.

338 Ebn-e Sirin was a famous Muslim scholar and interpreter of dreams. Born in Basra, he lived in the late 7th and early 8th centuries.

339 These two men were renowned for their generosity. Hâtem was a 6th-century pre-Islamic Arab poet and Afshin a 9th-century Persian general at the Abbasid court of the caliph Mo'tasem.

340 The original line is more complex and uses the names of two letters with

no diacritical marks (*vâv* and *hâ*) in the Arabo-Persian alphabet to indicate poverty, and then the names of two letters with diacritical marks (*sin* e *shin*) in the same alphabet to indicate wealth.

341 *Dugh* is a beverage made from yogurt, water and salt; here it is an allusion to spermatic fluid.

342 The reference is to anal penetration: see note 302.

343 Suzani 1959: 73–75.

344 Black is the representative colour of the Abbasid dynasty.

345 Silver and gold are two metaphors connected to sexual activity: the first stands for sperm and the second for faeces (explaining, in the latter case, the 'street sweeper's trade': see notes 302 and 342).

346 For musk see note 98. The allusion here is to the black colour of the musk (the pubic hair).

347 When numbers are represented by using certain configurations of the fingers (according to the rules of the *'aqd-e anâmel*/counting on fingers), ninety recalls the shape of the anus and twenty that of the vagina.

348 Ebn-e Yamin 1965: 114. Cutting off the head of the penis is an allusion to circumcision.

349 For the Magi see note 167.

350 For the *mehrâb* see note 242.

351 'Obeyd 1999: 201–203.

352 The following two poems are replies to two ghazals by Hâfez (Hâfez 1983: 22, 330), whose original words are in italics. On the technique of this kind of reply see Akhavân Sâles 1995; Nikubakht 2001: 99–118.

353 For musk see note 98.

354 Boshâq 1981: 35.

355 For Solomon and the ring see note 164.

356 The reference is to Mâni: see note 221.

357 Qâri 1886: 57.

358 'Obeyd 1999: 224. The hemistichs in italics come from a ghazal by Sa'di (Sa'di 1995: 505).

359 'Obeyd 1999: 229. The second and fourth hemistichs form the beginning of a famous *qaside* by Rudaki (Nezâmi-ye 'Aruzi 1967: 52). The Muliyân brook was in Bukhara. Rudaki mentions it to make the Samanid sovereign Nasr II (914–943) homesick and so convince him to return to Bukhara and give up the pleasures of his country retreat at Herat.

360 The reference to Mo'ezzi is based on the last line of the poem, but we have not found the work referred to in the printed edition of Mo'ezzi's divan (Mo'ezzi 1939). For some examples of Suzani's numerous replies to Sanâ'i see Akhavân Sâles 1995: 30–34.

361 Suzani 1959: 28–30.

362 See notes 302, 342 and 345.

363 Fereydun is a Persian epic hero. In the *Shâhnâme*, Ferdowsi tells how he managed to overcome the demon Zahhâk, who is mentioned in the following line.

364 Zahhâk is a legendary demonic creature, who, as narrated in the *Shâhnâme*, usurped and ruled for a while the ancient Persian kingdom. This creature has a monstrous appearance with, on his shoulders, two snakes who feed off human brains. This line is a kind of obscene 'fantastic etiology' concerning the snakes on the shoulders of the evil Zahhâk.

365 For Rostam see note 154.

366 Esfandiyâr is a Persian epic hero whose deeds are narrated by Ferdowsi in the *Shâhnâme*. He was killed in battle by Rostam.

367 The male member takes the place of the sun since, according to a legend, the sun's rays have the power to change stones into rubies.

368 According to Islamic law, adultery is a sin punishable by stoning to death. In this case stoning is a reference to the sexual act.

369 The poet's member is exalted through a sort of implied syllogism: given that the wood of plane trees is described by poets as self-inflammable and that his penis also catches fire by itself, the penis therefore is like a plane tree.

370 Anvari and Suzani, like Serâj-e Qomri, mentioned below, are referred to because they are leading authors of obscene poetry (some of their poems have been translated in this anthology).

371 This is the same judge whose penis is celebrated by Anvari in a short *masnavi* (see note 62).

372 Mohammad ebn-e Badr-e Jâjarmi 1959: 906–909 (in this source the poet is mentioned with a less well-known version of his name: Ebn-e Bahâ). The poem by Kamâl od-Din to which Pur-e Bahâ replied is in Kamâl od-Din's divan (Kamâl od-Din 1970: 115–118). The two poems have many rhyme-words in common. It should be noted, in particular, that the last rhyme-word (*ruzgâr*/'age') in Pur-e Bahâ's poem is the first rhyme-word in Kamâl od-Din's poem and the rhyme-word (*biqarâr*/'restless') of the second hemistich of the first line in Pur-e Bahâ's poem occurs in a simplified form (*qarâr*/'agreement') in the last line of Kamâl od-Din's poem. Moreover, the two poems also share a hemistich (the second one of line 32 in Pur-e Bahâ's poem and of line 13 in Kamâl od-Din's poem).

Biographies of the Poets

373 In drafting the biographical notes I have mainly referred to the following texts: Bausani 1960; de Blois 1992; de Blois 1994; Dabirsiyâqi 1976; Dabirsiyâqi 1977; Edârechi Gilâni 1991; Foruzânfar 1979; Halabi 1998; Kâseb 1991; Mazâher-e Mosaffâ 1956; Modabberi 1991; Nikubakht 2001; Rypka 1968; Safâ 1954; Shamisâ 2002. I have also consulted major reference works such as *Loghatnâme-ye Dehkhodâ* 1946 and *Encyclopædia Iranica* 1982–, and, in some cases, the prefaces to the individual divans.

Bibliography

Akhavân Sâles 1995: M. Akhavân Sâles, *Naqize o Naqizesâzân*, Tehran, 1995/1374.

ʿAmʿaq n.d.: ʿAmʿaq, *Divân*, edited by S. Nafisi, Tehran, n.d.

Amin Ahmad n.d.: Amin Ahmad-e Râzi, *Haft Eqlim*, edited by J. Fâzel, 3 vols., [Tehran], n.d.

Anvari 1959: Anvari, *Divân*, edited by S. Nafisi, [Tehran], 1959/1337.

ʿÂref 1976: ʿÂref-e Ardabili, *Farhâdnâme*, edited by ʿA. Âzar, [Tehran], 1976/2535 Imp.

Asadi 1940: Asadi, *Loghat-e Fors*, edited by ʿA. Eqbâl, Tehran, 1940–1941/1319.

Asadi 1977: Asadi, *Loghat-e Fors*, edited by M. Dabirsiyâqi, 2nd edn, [Tehran], 1977/1356.

Asir od-Din 1958: Asir od-Din-e Akhsikati, *Divân*, edited by R. Homâyun-Farrokh, Tehran, 1958/1337.

Askari n.d.: S.H. Askari, "Wit and Humour in the Works of Amir Khusrau", in *Life, Times and Works of Amir Khusrau Dehlavi*, New Dehli, n.d., pp. 146–166.

ʿAttâr 1963: ʿAttâr, *Manteq ot-Teyr*, edited by S.S. Gowharin, Tehran, 1963/1342.

ʿAttâr 2007: ʿAttâr, *Mosibatnâme*, edited by M.R. Shafiʿi Kadkani, 2nd edn, Tehran, 2007–2008/1386.

Âzar 1957: Lotf ʿAli Beyg Âzar-e Beygdeli, *Âteshkade*, edited by H. Sâdât-Nâseri, 3 vols., [Tehran], 1957–1962/1336–1340.

Âzar 1958: Lotf ʿAli Beyg Âzar-e Beygdeli, *Âteshkade*, edited by S.J. Shahidi, [Tehran], 1958/1337.

Bausani 1960: A. Bausani, *Letteratura neopersiana*, in A. Pagliaro and A. Bausani, *Storia della letteratura persiana*, Milan, 1960, pp. 149–876 (reprint: La Sapienza orientale-ristampe, Rome, 2011).

Behzâdi Anduhjerdi 1999: H. Behzâdi Anduhjerdi, *Tanz o Tanzpardâzi dar Irân*, Tehran, 1999/1378.

Behzâdi Anduhjerdi 2004: H. Behzâdi Anduhjerdi, *Tanzpardâzân-e Irân: az Âghâz tâ Pâyân-e Dowre-ye Qâjâr*, Tehran, 2004/1383.

Bertel's 1960: E. Bertel's, *Izbrannye Trudy, Istorija Persidsko-tadzhikskoĭ Literatury*, Moscow, 1960.

Bertel's 1988: E. Bertel's, *Izbrannye Trudy, Istorija Literatury i Kul'tury Irana*, Moscow, 1988.

Beyhaqi 1945: Abu 'l-Fazl Mohammad Beyhaqi, *Târikh-e Beyhaqi*, edited by ʿA.A. Fayyâz and Q. Ghani, Tehran, 1945–1946/1324.

Bible 2011: *Holy Bible. King James Version*, HarperCollins, London, 2011.

de Blois 1992: F. de Blois, *Persian Literature*, Vol. V, part 1, London, 1992.

de Blois 1994: F. de Blois, *Persian Literature*, Vol. V, part 2, London, 1994.

Boshâq 1981: Boshâq, *Divân-e Mowlânâ Boshâq Hallâj-e Shirâzi Mashhur be-Sheykh Atʿeme*, edited by M. Habib-e Esfahâni, 2nd edn, Shiraz, 1981/1360.

Dabirsiyâqi 1976: M. Dabirsiyâqi, *Ganj-e Bâzyâfte*, 2nd edn, Tehran, 1976/2535 Imp.

Dabirsiyâqi 1977: M. Dabirsiyâqi, *Pishâhangân-e Sheʿr-e Pârsi*, 2nd edn, Tehran, 1977/2536 Imp.

Dorri 1965: J. Dorri, *Persidskaya Satiricheskaya Poeziya*, Moscow, 1965.

Dowlatshâh 1987: Dowlatshâh-e Samarkandi, *Tazkerat osh-Shoʿarâ*, edited by M. Ramazâni, 2nd edn, Tehran, 1987/1366.

Ebn-e Yamin 1965: Ebn-e Yamin, *Divân-e Ashʿâr*, edited by H. Bâstâni-Râd, [Tehran], [1965/1344].

Edârechi Gilâni 1991: A. Edârechi Gilâni, *Shâʿerân-e Hamʿasr-e Rudaki*, Tehran, 1991/1370.

Encyclopædia Iranica 1982–: *Encyclopædia Iranica*, edited by E. Yarshater, Costa Mesa, 1982–; also www.iranicaonline.org.

Enju 1980: Jamâl od-Din Hoseyn Enju, *Farhang-e Jahângiri*, edited by R. ʿAfifi, 2nd edn, 2 vols., Mashhad, 1980–1981/1359.

Farghâni 1985: Farghâni, *Divân*, edited by Z. Safâ, 2nd edn, Tehran, 1985–1986/1364.

Ferdowsi 1990: Ferdowsi, *Shâhnâme*, edited by J. Mohl, 3rd edn, 7 vols. in 4, Tehran, 1990–1991/1369.

Floor 2008: W. Floor, *A Social History of Sexual Relations in Iran*, Washington, 2008.

Föllmer 2008: K. Föllmer, *Satire in Iran von 1990 bis 2000, Eine Analyse exemplarischer Texte*, Wiesbaden, 2008.

Foruzânfar 1979: B. Foruzânfar, *Sokhan o Sokhanvarân*, 3rd edn, Tehran, 1979/1358.

van Gelder 1988: G.J. van Gelder, *The Bad and the Ugly; Attitudes toward Invective Poetry (Hijâ') in Classical Arabic Literature*, Leiden, 1988.

van Gelder 1992: G.J. van Gelder, "Mixtures of Jest and Earnest in Classical

Arabic Literature", *Journal of Arabic Literature* XXIII, 1992, part 2, July, pp. 83–108; part 3, November, pp. 169–190.

van Gelder 1995: G.J. van Gelder, "Street-Arabs, Satire and the Status of Poetry", in *Proceedings of the 14th Congress of the Union Européenne des Arabisants et Islamisants*, part 2, Budapest, 1995, pp. 121–132.

Griffin 1994: D. Griffin, *Satire, A Critical Reintroduction*, Lexington, 1994.

Hâfez 1983: Hâfez, *Divân*, edited by P.N. Khânlari, 2nd edn, 2 vols., Tehran, 1983–1984/1362.

Halabi 1980: ʿA.A. Halabi, *The Development of Humour and Satire in Persia with Special Reference to ʿUbaid Zâkânî*, Ph.D. diss., Edinburgh, 1980.

Halabi 1985: ʿA.A. Halabi, *Moqaddame-i bar Tanz o Shukhtabʿi dar Irân*, Tehran, 1985/1364.

Halabi 1998: ʿA.A. Halabi, *Tanz o Shukhtabʿi dar Irân o Jahân-e Eslâm*, [Tehran], 1998/1377.

Hedâyat 1957: Rezâ Qoli Khân Hedâyat, *Majmaʿ ol-Fosahâ*, edited by Mazâher-e Mosaffâ, 2 vols. in 6, [Tehran], 1957–1962/1336–1340.

Highet 1962: G. Highet, *The Anatomy of Satire*, Princeton, 1962.

Hodgart 1969: M. Hodgart, *Satire*, New York, 1969.

Hoffmann 1990: B. Hoffmann, "Von falschen Asketen und 'unfrommen' Stiftungen", in *Proceedings of the First European Conference of Iranian Studies* (held in Turin, September 7th–11th 1987), edited by G. Gnoli and A. Panaino, 2 vols., Rome, 1990, II, pp. 409–485.

Homâm 1972: Homâm, *Divân*, edited by R. ʿEyvazi, Tabriz, 1972/1351.

Jabali 1977: ʿAbd ol-Vâseʿ-e Jabali, *Divân*, edited by Z. Safâ, 2nd edn, Tehran, 1977/2536 Imp.

Jamâl od-Din 1941: Jamâl od-Din, *Divân*, edited by H.V. Dastgerdi, [Tehran], 1941/1320.

Jâmi 1999a: Jâmi, *Divân*, edited by A. Afsahzâd, 2 vols., Tehran, 1999/1378.

Jâmi 1999b: Jâmi, *Masnavi-ye Haft Owrang*, edited by J. Dâd-ʿAlishâh, A. Jânfadâ, Z. Ahrâri, H.A. Tarbiyyat and A. Afsahzâd, 2 vols., Tehran, 1999/1378.

Javadi 1988: H. Javadi, *Satire in Persian Literature*, London-Toronto, 1988.

Kamâl od-Din 1970: Kamâl od-Din, *Divân*, edited by H. Bahr ol-ʿOlumi, Tehran, 1970/1348.

Kâseb 1991: ʿA. Kâseb, *Chashmandâz-e Târikhi-ye Hajv*, 2nd edn, [Tehran], 1991/1369.

Kavir 1997: M. Kavir, *Târikh-e Tanz dar Irân*, Stockholm, 1997.

Key Kâʾus 1973: Key Kâʾus ebn-e Eskandar, *Qâbusnâme*, edited by Gh. Yusofi, 2nd edn, Tehran, 1973–1974/1352.

Khâju 1957: Khâju, *Divân-e Ashʿâr*, edited by A. Soheyli Khânsâri, [Tehran], [1957/1336].

Khâqâni 1937: Khâqâni, *Divân*, edited by ʿA. ʿAbd or-Rasuli, [Tehran], 1937–1938/1316.

Khâqâni 1978: Khâqâni, *Masnavi-ye Tohfat ol-ʿErâqeyn*, edited by Y. Qarib, 2nd edn, Tehran, 1978/2537 Imp.

Khâqâni 1989: Khâqâni, *Divân*, edited by Z. Sajjâdi, 3rd edn, Tehran, 1989–1990/1368.

Khâqâni 1997: Khâqâni, *Divân*, edited by M.J. Kazzâzi, 2 vols., Tehran, 1997/1375.

Khayyâm 1931: ʿOmar Khayyâm, *Robâʿiyyât*, edited by A. Eʿtesâmzâde, Tehran, 1931/1310.

Khayyâm 1959: ʿOmar Khayyâm, *Robâʿiyyât*, edited by R.M. Aliev and M.N.O. Osmanov, 2 vols., Moscow, 1959.

Koran 1955: *The Koran Interpreted. A Translation by A.J. Arberry*, New York, 1955.

Lâmeʿi 1976: Lâmeʿi, *Divân*, edited by M. Dabirsiyâqi, 2nd edn, Tehran, 1976/2535 Imp.

Loghatnâme-ye Dehkhodâ 1946: *Loghatnâme-ye Dehkhodâ*, founded by ʿA.A. Dehkhodâ and continued by M. Moʿin et al., Tehran, 1946–1981/1325–1360.

Mahjub 1967: M.J. Mahjub, *Sabk-e Khorâsâni dar Sheʿr-e Fârsi*, Tehran, 1967/1345.

Manuchehri 1977: Manuchehri, *Divân*, edited by M. Dabirsiyâqi, 4th edn, Tehran, 1977/1356.

Marzolph 1992: U. Marzolph, *Arabia ridens*, 2 vols., Frankfurt am Main, 1992.

Masʿud-e Saʿd 1939: Masʿud-e Saʿd, *Divân*, edited by R. Yâsemi, Tehran, 1939/1318.

Mazâher-e Mosaffâ 1956: Mazâher-e Mosaffâ, *Pâsdârân-e Sokhan*, Tehran, [1956/1335].

Meier 1963: F. Meier, *Die schöne Mahsatî; ein Beitrag zur Geschichte des persischen Vierzeilers*, band I, Wiesbaden, 1963.

Meier 2005: F. Meier, *Die schöne Mahsatî; band 2, Der Volksroman über Mahsatî und Amîr Ahmad*, edited by G. Schubert and R. Würsch, Leiden-Boston, 2005.

Meisami 2003: J.S. Meisami, *Structure and Meaning in Medieval Arabic and Persian Poetry: Orient Pearls*, London, 2003.

Modabberi 1991: M. Modabberi, *Sharh-e Ahvâl o Ashʿâr-e Shâʿerân-e Bidivân dar Qarnhâ-ye 3/4/5 Hejri-ye Qamari*, [Tehran], 1991/1370.

Moʿezzi 1939: Moʿezzi, *Divân*, edited by ʿA. Eqbâl, [Tehran], 1939–1940/1318.

Mohammad ebn-e Badr-e Jâjarmi 1959: Mohammad ebn-e Badr-e Jâjarmi,

Mo'nes ol-Ahrâr fi Daqâ'eq ol-Ash'âr, edited by M.S. Tabibi, 2 vols., [Tehran], 1959–1971/1337–1350.

Mojir od-Din 1979: Mojir od-Din, *Divân*, edited by M. Âbâdi, Tabriz, 1979/1358.

Mokhtâri 1962: Mokhtâri, *Divân*, edited by J. Homâ'i, Tehran, 1962/1341.

Mo'tamen 1967: Z. Mo'tamen, *She'r o Adab-e Fârsi*, [Tehran], 1967/1346.

Nâser-e Khosrow 1956: Nâser-e Khosrow, *Divân*, edited by N. Taqavi, Tehran, 1956/1335.

Nâser-e Khosrow 1986: Nâser-e Khosrow, *Divân*, edited by M. Minovi and M. Mohaqqeq, Tehran, 1986/1365.

Nasrollâh Monshi 1964: Abu 'l-Ma'âli Nasrollâh Monshi, *Tarjome-ye Kalile o Demne*, edited by M. Minovi, Tehran, 1964–1965/1343.

Navâ'i 1984: Mir Nezâm od-Din 'Ali Shir Navâ'i, *Tazkere-ye Majâles on-Nafâ'es*, edited by 'A.A. Hekmat, Tehran, 1984–1985/1363.

Nazir Ahmad 1991: Nazir Ahmad, "Gozâresh-e Mokhtasar-i darbâre-ye Hajv-nevisi-ye Ferdowsi", *Qand-e Pârsi* 2–3, 1991/1370, pp. 1–20.

Nesâ'i 1960: Tâj od-Din-e Nesâ'i, "Kârnâme-ye Owqâf", edited by I. Afshâr, *Farhang-e Irânzamin* VIII, 1960/1339, pp. 5–22.

Nezâm ol-Molk 1962: Nezâm ol-Molk, *Siyar ol-Moluk (Siyâsatnâme)*, edited by H. Darke, Tehran, 1962/1340.

Nezâmi-ye 'Aruzi 1967: Nezâmi-ye 'Aruzi, *Chahâr Maqâle*, edited by M. Mo'in, 8th edn, Tehran, 1967–1968/1346.

Nezâmi-ye Ganjavi 1954: Nezâmi-ye Ganjavi, *Leylâ o Majnun*, edited by V. Dastgerdi, 2nd edn, n.p., 1954/1333.

Nezâri 1992: Nezâri, *Divân*, edited by Mazâher-e Mosaffâ, Tehran, 1992/1371.

Nikubakht 2001: N. Nikubakht, *Hajv dar She'r-e Fârsi, Naqd o Barrasi-ye She'r-e Hajvi az Âghâz tâ 'Asr-e 'Obeyd*, Tehran, 2001/1380.

'Obeyd 1999: 'Obeyd, *Kolliyyât*, edited by M.J. Mahjub, New York, 1999.

'Owfi 1903: Mohammad 'Owfi, *Lobâb ol-Albâb*, edited by E.G. Browne and M.M. Qazvini, 2 vols., London-Leiden, 1903–1906.

Owhadi 1996: Owhadi, *Kolliyyât*, edited by S. Nafisi, 2nd edn, Tehran, 1996–1997/1375.

Qamar 1984: Qamar, *Divân*, edited by T. Binesh, Mashhad, 1984–1985/1363.

Qâri 1886: Qâri, *Divân-e Albese*, edited by M. Habib-e Esfahâni, Constantinople, 1886/1303.

Qazvini 1953: M.M. Qazvini, *Bist Maqâle*, 2nd edn, 2 vols., [Tehran], 1953/1332.

Qomri 1989: Qomri, *Divân*, edited by Y. Shokri, Tehran, 1989–1990/1368.

Râduyâni 1949: Râduyâni, *Tarjomân ol-Balâghe*, edited by A. Âtesh, Istanbul, 1949.

Rastegâr-e Fasâyi 1993: M. Rastegâr-e Fasâyi, *Anvâʿ-e Sheʿr-e Fârsi*, Shiraz, 1993–1994/1372.

Râvandi 1921: Mohammad Râvandi, *Râhat os-Sodur o Âyat os-Sorur*, edited by M. Eqbâl, Leiden-London, 1921.

Rumi 1925: Rumi, *Masnavi-ye Mʿanavi*, edited by R.A. Nicholson, 8 vols., London-Leiden, 1925–1940.

Rypka 1968: J. Rypka et al., *History of Iranian Literature*, Dordrecht, 1968.

Saʿdi 1995: Saʿdi, *Kolliyyât az ruy-e Noskhe-ye Tashihshode-ye M.ʿA. Forughi*, Tehran, 1995–1996/1374.

Safâ 1954: Z. Safâ, *Târikh-e Adabiyyât dar Irân*, 5 vols. in 8, Tehran, 1954–1992/1332–1370.

Salâhi 2003: ʿO. Salâhi, *Khandesâzân o Khandepardâzân*, Tehran, 2003–2004/1382.

Salmân n.d.: Salmân, *Kolliyyât*, edited by Avestâ, Tehran, n.d.

Sâm Mirzâ n.d.: Sâm Mirzâ, *Tazkere-ye Tohfe-ye Sâmi*, edited by R. Homâyun-Farrokh, [Tehran], n.d.

Sanâʾi 1981: Sanâʾi, *Masnavihâ*, edited by M.T. Modarres-e Razavi, 2nd edn, Tehran, 1981–1982/1360.

Sanâʾi 1983: Sanâʾi, *Divân*, edited by M.T. Modarres-e Razavi, 3rd edn, [Tehran], 1983–1984/1362.

Sanâʾi 1989: Sanâʾi, *Hadiqat ol-Haqiqe o Shariʿat ot-Tariqe*, edited by M.T. Modarres-e Razavi, Tehran, 1989/1368.

Shamisâ 2002: S. Shamisâ, *Shâhedbâzi dar Adabiyyât-e Fârsi*, Tehran, 2002/1381.

Shams-e Qeys 1981: Shams od-Din Mohammad ebn-e Qeys or-Râzi (Shams-e Qeys), *Al-Moʿjam fi Maʿâyir Ashʿâr ol-ʿAjam*, edited by M.M. Qazvini and M.T. Modarres-e Razavi, 3rd edn, Tehran, [1981/1360].

Shebli Noʿmâni 1984: Shebli Noʿmâni, *Sheʿr ol-ʿAjam yâ Târikh-e Shoʿarâ o Adabiyyât-e Irân*, translated by M.T. Fakhr-e Dâʿi-ye Gilâni, 2nd edn, 5 vols. in 2, Tehran, 1984–1985/1363.

Skalmowski 1999: W. Skalmowski, "Humour in Rumi's *Ghazals*", *Orientalia Lovaniensia Periodica*, 30, 1999 [2001], pp. 83–95.

Sprachman 1981: P. Sprachman, *The Comic Works of ʿUbayd-i Zâkâni: a Study of Medieval Persian Bawdy, Verbal Aggression, and Satire*, Ph.D. diss., Chicago, 1981.

Sprachman 1988: P. Sprachman, "Persian Satire, Parody and Burlesque: A General Notion of Genre", in *Persian Literature*, edited by E. Yarshater, [Albany, N.Y.], 1988, pp. 226–248.

Sprachman 1995: P. Sprachman, *Suppressed Persian: An Anthology of Forbidden Literature*, Costa Mesa, 1995.

Suzani 1959: Suzani, *Divân*, edited by N. Shâh-Hoseyni, [Tehran], 1959/1338.

Test 1991: G.A. Test, *Satire: Spirit and Art*, Tampa, 1991.

Vatvât 1960: Vatvât, *Divân*, edited by S. Nafisi, Tehran, 1960–1961/1339.

Yârshâter 1955: E. Yârshâter, *She'r-e Fârsi dar 'Ahd-e Shâhrokh*, Tehran, 1955/1334.

Zahir od-Din 1982: Zahir od-Din-e Fâryâbi, *Divân*, edited by H.Sh.A. Shirâzi, 2nd edn, [Tehran], 1982/1361.

Zarrinkub 1982: 'A. Zarrinkub, *Naqd-e Adabi*, 3rd edn, 2 vols., Tehran, 1982–1983/1361.

Zarrinkub 1992: 'A. Zarrinkub, *She'r-e Bidorugh, She'r-e Bineqâb*, reprint, n.p., 1992–1993/1371.

Zhukovskiĭ 1902: V. Zhukovskiĭ, *Obrazcy Persidskavo Narodnavo Tvorchestva*, Saint Petersburg, 1902.

Zipoli 1994: R. Zipoli, "Oscenità poetiche neopersiane: due *tarjî'-band* sulla masturbazione", *Annali di Ca' Foscari*, XXXIII, 3 (serie orientale 25), 1994, pp. 249–291.

Zipoli 1995: R. Zipoli, "I Carmina Priapea di Sûzanî", *Annali di Ca' Foscari*, XXXIV, 3 (serie orientale 26), 1995, pp. 205–256.

Zipoli 1996: R. Zipoli, "Elementi osceni nella lessicografia neopersiana", *Annali di Ca' Foscari*, XXXV, 3 (serie orientale 27), 1996, pp. 249–289.

Zipoli 1997: R. Zipoli, "Le *Khabîthât* oscene di Sa'dî", *Annali di Ca' Foscari*, XXXVI, 3 (serie orientale 28), 1997, pp. 179–214.

Zipoli 2001: R. Zipoli, "The obscene Sanâ'i", *Persica*, XVII, 2001, pp. 173–194.

Zipoli 2002: R. Zipoli, "Il Khâqâni polemico", in *Studi e scritti in memoria di Marzio Marzaduri*, edited by G. Pagani-Cesa and O. Obuchova, Eurasiatica 66, Venice, 2002, pp. 457–482.

Zipoli 2006: R. Zipoli, "Anvari, a master of obscene verse", in *Studies on the Poetry of Anvari*, edited by D. Meneghini, Eurasiatica 74, Venice, 2006, pp. 149–172.

Zipoli 2008: R. Zipoli, "Rûmî, autore di versi osceni", in *Scritti in onore di Biancamaria Scarcia Amoretti*, edited by D. Bredi, L. Capezzone, W. Dahmash and L. Rostagno, 3 vols., Rome, 2008, Vol. III, pp. 1237–1246.

Zipoli 2010: R. Zipoli, "'Lui è turco ed io sono persiano': una satira religiosa di Jâmi", in *Sûzişât-i mü'ellefe, Contaminazioni e spigolature turcologiche, Scritti in onore di Giampiero Bellingeri*, edited by V. Costantini and M. Kappler, Crocetta del Montello, 2010, pp. 401–409.

Zipoli 2011: R. Zipoli, "Obscene vocabulary in Steingass's dictionary", in *The Persian language in history*, edited by M. Maggi and P. Orsatti, Wiesbaden, 2011, pp. 297–305.

Zipoli 2015: R. Zipoli, "Obscene Persian Poetry: tradition and innovation", in *Shâ'er-e Târikh/The Rhapsodist of History*, in Commemoration of M.E. Bastani Parizi, supervised by Hamide and Hamid Bastani Parizi, Tehran, 2015/1394, pp. 13–33.

Index of Names, Places and Works

Iranian Studies Series

J.C. Bürgel & C. van Ruymbeke (eds.)
Nizāmī: A Key to the Treasure of the Hakim
ISBN 978 90 8728 097 0

J. Coumans
The Rubáiyát of Omar Khayyám. An Updated Bibliography
ISBN 978 90 8728 096 3

N. Fozi
Reclaiming the Faravahar: Zoroastrian Survival in Contemporary Tehran
ISBN 978 90 8728 214 1

F. Lewis & S. Sharma (eds.)
The Necklace of the Pleiades. 24 Essays on Persian Literature, Culture and Religion
ISBN 978 90 8728 091 8

M.A. Nematollahi Mahani
The Holy Drama. Persian Passion Plays in Modern Iran
ISBN 978 90 8728 115 1

C. Pérez González
Local Portraiture. Through the Lens of the 19th-Century Iranian Photographers
ISBN 978 90 8728 156 4

L. Rahimi Bahmany
Mirrors of Entrapment of Emancipation: Forugh Farrokhzad and Sylvia Plath
ISBN 978 90 8728 224 0

R. Rahmoni & G. van den Berg
The Epic of Barzu as Narrated by Jura Kamal
ISBN 978 90 8728 116 8

A. Sedighi
Agreement Restrictions in Persian
ISBN 978 90 8728 093 2

A. Sedighi
Persian in Use: An Elementary Textbook of Language and Culture
ISBN 978 90 8728 217 2

A.A. Seyed-Gohrab
Courtly Riddles. Enigmatic Embellishments in Early Persian Poetry
ISBN 978 90 8728 087 1

A.A. Seyed-Gohrab (ed.)
The Great Umar Khayyam: A Global Reception of the Rubáiyat
ISBN 978 90 8728 157 1

A.A. Seyed-Gohrab & S.R.M. McGlinn (eds.)
One Word—Yak Kaleme. 19th-Century Persian Treatise Introducing Western Codified Law
ISBN 978 90 8728 089 5

A.A. Seyed-Gohrab & S.R.M. McGlinn (eds.)
Safina Revealed. A Compendium of Persian Literature in 14th-Century Tabriz
ISBN 978 90 8728 088 8

A.A. Seyed-Gohrab, F. Doufikar-Aerts & S. McGlinn (eds.)
Embodiments of Evil: Gog and Magog. Interdisciplinary Studies of the 'Other' in Literature & Internet Texts
ISBN 978 90 8728 090 1

P. Shabani-Jadidi
Processing Compound Verbs in Persian: A Psycholinguistic Approach to Complex Predicates
ISBN 978 90 8728 208 0

B. Solati
The Reception of Ḥāfiẓ: The Sweet Poetic Language of Ḥāfiẓ in Nineteenth and Twentieth Century Persia
ISBN 978 90 8728 197 7

S. Tabatabai
Father of Persian Verse. Rudaki and his Poetry
ISBN 978 90 8728 092 5

K. Talattof & A.A. Seyed-Gohrab (eds.)
Conflict and Development in Iranian Film
ISBN 978 90 8728 169 4

Forthcoming titles in the *Iranian Studies Series*:

J.T.P. de Bruijn, *The Journey of the Faithful to the Place of Return. A Persian Allegory on the Development of the Human Soul by Sanâ'i of Ghazna, Founding Father of Persian Sufism*

J.T.L. Cheung, *The Nartic Epic Tradition. Remnants of Iranian Lore from the Caucasus*

S.R.M. McGlinn, *Abdul-Baha's Sermon on the Art of Governance*

Printed in the United States
by Baker & Taylor Publisher Services